WEAPON

THE MARTINI-HENRY RIFLE

STEPHEN MANNING

Series Editor Martin Pegler

OSPREY PUBLISHING
Bloomsbury Publishing Plc

Kemp House, Chawley Park, Oxford OX2 9PH, UK
29 Earlsfort Terrace, Dublin 2, Ireland
1385 Broadway, 5th Floor, New York, NY 10018, USA
Email: info@ospreypublishing.com
www.ospreypublishing.com

OSPREY is a trademark of Osprey Publishing Ltd

First published in Great Britain in 2013

© Osprey Publishing Ltd, 2013

Transferred to digital print in 2023

A catalogue record for this book is available from the
British Library.

Print ISBN: 978 1 78096 506 2
ePDF: 978 1 78096 507 9
ePub: 978 1 78096 508 6

Index by Zoe Ross
Typeset in Sabon and Univers
Battlescenes by Peter Dennis
Originated by PDQ Media, Bungay, UK
Printed and bound in India by Replika Press Private Ltd.

23 24 25 26 27   15 14 13 12 11 10

The Woodland Trust
Osprey Publishing supports the Woodland Trust, the UK's leading
woodland conservation charity.

www.ospreypublishing.com
To find out more about our authors and books visit our website.
Here you will find extracts, author interviews, details of
forthcoming events and the option to sign-up for our newsletter.

Acknowledgements
In collecting photographs for this book I have been overwhelmed
by the kindness and generosity of so many individuals. I would
particularly like to thank: Ian Knight; Adrian Greaves; Robert
and Jonathan Hope; Al Petrillo; Robin Jenkins of the
Leicestershire Records Office; Richard Dabb of the National
Army Museum; Jesper Ericsson of The Gordon Highlanders
Museum; Andrew and Mrs Betty Stadden; Mrs Christine Pullen
of The Rifles Museum (Winchester); Dan Allen, Andrew Kilsby
and Ron Sheeley of the Victorian Military Society; Edward
Garcia from the Soldiers of the Queen website; Simon Cook of
The Rifles Museum (Berkshire and Wiltshire); and Stephen
Maggs of Christ College, Brecon.

Ian Skennerton was helpful both with advice and in granting
his permission to use some of his images. I would like to thank
Ian Beckett for his permission to use some details from an article
he has written on the Martini-Henry that is soon to be published.
Neil Aspinshaw has been generous in giving of both his advice
and time and I am so thankful to him for allowing me to fulfil an
ambition to fire a Martini-Henry. Neil recently formed the
Martini-Henry Society and intends to establish a website in the
near future. Spare parts for the Martini-Henry can be purchased
via Neil or Peter Dyson at <www.peterdyson.co.uk>.

Finally I would like to thank my wife, Michaela, for her proof-
reading skills and her patience and my two sons, Alexander and
Dominic, for putting up with their rather obsessive father. To
understand the development of the Martini-Henry was a
complex, and at times, confusing exercise. Naturally, any errors
in the text are solely my responsibility.

Author's dedication
To M.A.F. Hunter

Editor's note
For ease of comparison please refer to the following
conversion table:

1 mile = 1.6km
1yd = 0.9m
1ft = 0.3m
1in = 2.54cm/25.4mm
1lb = 0.45kg
1 grain = 64.8mg

Artist's note
Readers may care to note that the original paintings from which
the battlescenes of this book were prepared are available for
private sale. All reproduction copyright whatsoever is retained
by the Publishers. All enquiries should be addressed to:

Peter Dennis, 'Fieldhead', The Park, Mansfield,
Nottinghamshire NG18 2AT, UK

Email magie.h@ntlworld.com

The Publishers regret that they can enter into no correspondence
upon this matter.

Image acknowledgements
Front cover images are © Jonathan R. Hope (top)
and Osprey Publishing (bottom)

CONTENTS

INTRODUCTION

The second half of the 19th century witnessed many crucial innovations in military technology, but perhaps the most significant was the transition from muzzle-loading to breech-loading rifles during the 1860s, which dramatically widened the power gap between Western and non-Western peoples. War is, and always has been, a huge spur to technological advancement. This was most certainly true in the year 1864, when the governments of Europe and America were shocked into action by the events of the Danish–Prussian War. In a short and decisive campaign the Prussians, armed with the breech-loading 15.4mm (0.61in) M1841 Dreyse *Zündnadelgewehr* (Needle Gun), easily defeated the Danes with their inferior percussion-cap muzzle-loading arms. Prussian success was repeated in the Austro-Prussian War of 1866. Unlike muzzle-loading rifles, the Dreyse could be fired and reloaded while kneeling or prone, thus reducing the profile of the soldier and lessening the risk of death or injury, and the ease of loading their breech-loading rifles meant that the Prussian troops were able to fire seven times as fast as the Austrians (Headrick 1981: 97). This brief war was concluded at the decisive battle of Sadowa (aka Königgrätz) on 3 July 1866.

The lessons for military observers from other countries, including Britain, from these two impressive Prussian victories was that the breech-loading rifle would revolutionize the battlefield. All major powers entered an arms race which would see a rapid evolution in rifle technology. The French Army responded with a two-pronged approach. First came the adoption of the 11mm (0.43in) Fusil modèle 1866, known as the Chassepot after its inventor, a bolt-action gun that could be fired up to six times a minute and had an official range of 650yd, 300yd further than the Dreyse. Alongside the Chassepot, the French converted the old 18mm (0.71in) Minié muzzle-loading rifles to breech-loaders. Although both weapons saw service in the Franco-Prussian War of 1870, neither rifle was completely successful. Both fouled quickly and leaked hot gases at the breech (known as obturation), and the worse the fouling, the more they leaked. Under battlefield conditions French troops reported that fouling and leakage became so pronounced that they were forced to fire the rifles at arm's length to avoid being singed. Any accuracy such weapons might have possessed was thus annulled (Headrick 1981: 98).

The British reaction to the technological threat from breech-loading rifles was, initially, rapid. The Secretary of State for War, the Earl de Gray and Ripon, appointed an Ordnance Select Committee in early 1864, with the brief to 'report on the advisability of arming the infantry, either in whole or in part, with breech loading arms'. In its final report of July 1864, this committee, without reference to any particular form of breech-loading system, stated that it was in favour of arming the infantry wholly with breech-loaders. This decision was to result in the demise of the muzzle-loader in British service.

Unlike the French, however, the British had no breech-loading rifle available that could be readily adopted. The clear technological advantage that the both the French and Prussians now possessed over the British was somewhat nullified by the British decision to follow a similar path to the French Army and to convert the existing muzzle-loading .577in Pattern 1853 Enfield Rifle-Muskets then in service into breech-loading rifles. The conversion of the Enfield was undertaken by the adoption of a device designed by Jacob Snider of New York. A 2.5in length was cut away from the breech and into the trough a right-handed steel block was inserted. This consisted of a claw extractor which was incorporated into the breech

Men of the 1st Leicestershire on St Lucia, 1894, armed with either Mark III or Mark IV Martini-Henry rifles. (Courtesy of Leicestershire Records Office)

The Chassepot bolt-action rifle, which entered service in 1866, was the French Army's response to the success of the German Dreyse Needle Gun. The Chassepot could be fired up to six times a minute and its official range of 650yd was nearly double that of the Dreyse. Although a significant technological advance, the Chassepot had several faults, the most significant being that of rapid fouling of the barrel and leakage of hot gases, which made the rifle difficult to fire accurately for any prolonged period. (Rama/CC BY-SA 2.0 FR)

mechanism, with a striker operated by the original Enfield hammer. The extractor partially pulled the new centre-fire cartridge case out of the open breech, and was discarded by turning the rifle upside down with a swift arm movement. The rate of fire increased dramatically to about eight or nine rounds per minute, having formerly been three or four at best.

The British Army began to be equipped with this Snider-Enfield rifle in 1866. However, the weapon experienced similar problems of gas leakage and breech fouling to those found in both the Dreyse and the Chassepot. The Royal Laboratory at Woolwich, which conducted extensive tests on breech-loaders, realized that the weakness in the design, and the major factor affecting gas leakage and fouling, was the paper cartridge. Rapid-firing breechloaders and repeating rifles could only operate if the primer, powder and bullet were all contained in a cartridge. Paper cartridges, as in the British, French and German weapons, were too delicate and allowed gases to escape during firing, causing soldiers to keep their guns away from their face and thus reducing the accuracy of their aim. A metal cartridge would solve the problem.

In 1866–67 Colonel Edward M. Boxer of the Woolwich Arsenal developed a brass cartridge that held the bullet, powder and cap together; it was sturdy and waterproof and, best of all, sealed the breech during the explosion. This resulted in a flatter trajectory, allowing greater range. The range of the Snider-Enfield of 1867 was extraordinary – at over 1,000yd, it was three times that of the Dreyse and almost twice that of the Chassepot. Accuracy was also significantly improved, as the user was able to hold the rifle close to his face without fear of escaping gases.

The Snider-Enfield soon demonstrated its firepower and accuracy in a number of conflicts around the world. For example, during the Abyssinian campaign of 1867–68, the British, armed with Snider-Enfields, defeated the 7,000-strong army of Emperor Tewodros on the Aroghee Plain

(10 April 1868). For the most part the attackers were scythed down by carefully controlled Snider volley fire. Colonel Cameron, commanding 300 rifles of the 1/4th Regiment, ordered his men to hold their fire until the enemy approached to within 250yd. Cameron later wrote:

> Three hundred blue barrels came up together, and three hundred hammers clicked back to full cock. The burst of fire ran down the line with a noise like a great tearing of canvas and a wide gap appeared abruptly in the centre of the Abyssinian line as the storm of fire hit it. Hundreds went down at the first discharge and the whole line reeled. Theodore's fighting men, used only to muzzle-loaders, apparently anticipated a decent interval while the slow ritual of powder and ball, rod and cap was obeyed, but it was not granted them. (Quoted in Myatt 1970: 140)

The British were firing independently and by the time the more deliberate shots had fired their first rounds the quicker men were ready with their second. The fire was therefore continuous; six or eight rounds a minute, so that the line was probably producing 30 or 40 well-aimed shots each second – a remarkable figure.

Despite the Snider-Enfield's success, which would see it remain in service with the Indian Army well into the 1890s, the need to find a modern replacement was officially recognized on 22 October 1865, when the War Office issued an invitation to all 'Gunmakers and Others' requesting that proposals be submitted 'for breech-loading rifles, either repeating or not repeating, which may replace the present service rifles in future manufacture' (War Office 1868). The long, arduous and sometimes frustrating story of the Martini-Henry rifle had begun.

The Snider-Enfield was introduced in 1866, and was used by the British Army until it was superseded by the Martini-Henry; it remained in service with the Indian Army until the mid-1890s. The Snider-Enfield first saw action with British forces at the battle of Aroghee in Ethiopia on 10 April 1868. (National Firearms Museum, NRAmuseum.org)

DEVELOPMENT
A British breech-loader

While the German and French armies had been able to call upon the inventive skills of Messrs Dreyse and Chassepot, the British decided to adopt a very different approach. On 22 October 1865, the War Office invited rifle manufacturers to submit their designs in a 'Prize Competition'. The War Office provided a comprehensive list of criteria and technical specifications to be met; these included a weight limit of 9lb 5oz, without bayonet, and total length to be no more than 51in, as well as specific limits for recoil, fouling, accuracy and penetration. (The Snider-Enfield weighed 8lb 9oz and was 54.25in long, while the Dreyse was 142cm (55.9in) long and weighed 4.7kg (10lb 6oz); the Chassepot was 131cm (51.6in) long and weighed 4.6kg (10lb 2oz).) The decisions as to calibre and rifling were left to the individual manufacturer.

Incredibly, 104 rifles were received for consideration, with every inventor invited to explain their design and fire the weapon. A process of assessment and rejection continued throughout 1866–67 until, of the original submissions, only nine remained. This figure included rifles from the Remington and Peabody companies, the Swiss–Hungarian Friedrich von Martini (1833–97) and the Scot Alexander Henry (1828–94). All nine were subjected to numerous tests, including the exposure test in which a total of 100 rounds were fired during four consecutive days, with the rifles being kept dirty and exposed to the elements throughout. They were then left uncleaned for a further 14 days and nights, then fired again. Finally, each was disassembled and examined (Westwood 2005: 57).

The trials highlighted a number of problems with eight of the rifles. For example, the Remington's breech block frequently jammed and the Martini could only be fired once after the fortnight's exposure. However, the Henry's breech mechanism 'worked well throughout' (Westwood 2005: 58). Furthermore both the Martini and Remington rifles were

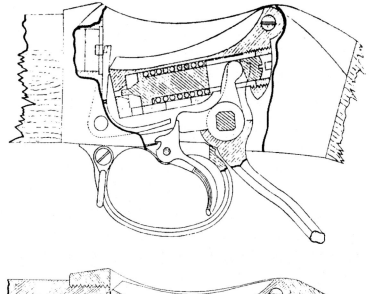

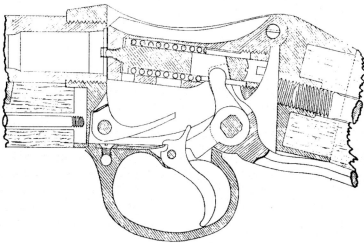

The Martini-Henry Mark II action mechanism, (above) open and cocked, and (below) closed and fired. The Mark II was the most widely mark of the Martini-Henry, and its mechanism was significantly improved over the Mark I. (Courtesy of Ian Skennerton)

eliminated from the 'rapidity of fire' test due to faulty cartridges. This test was jointly won by the Peabody and Henry rifles, which both demonstrated an impressive potential rate of fire of 16 rounds per minute. The War Office declared the Henry rifle to be the best of the weapons submitted, and duly awarded its inventor £600 for producing the rifle with the finest breech mechanism (Temple & Skennerton 1983: 22). The Martini was not considered satisfactory, although the Trials Committee did concede that the Martini's failings could be largely attributed to faults with its cartridges.

Although it had won the trial, the Trials Committee, concerned with the lack of accuracy displayed by the rifle, failed to recommend the adoption of the Henry rifle, or any of the other eight weapons, for general issue. Indeed the Committee concluded that the present Service rifle, the Snider-Enfield, 'performed well during several of the trials to which it was subjected, and proved itself in many respects an efficient military weapon' (Temple & Skennerton 1983: 23). In addition, the Committee expressed the hope that future trials would enable them to recommend the

Martini-Henry cartridges

Service Martini-Henry rifles used an adapted .450in cartridge developed by Colonel E.M. Boxer for use in the Snider-Enfield arms. The Boxer-Henry cartridge, technically the Mark III Boxer, emerged in August 1873. It was of relatively thin and soft rolled-brass sheeting, while the charge of 85 grains of black powder was an especially heavy one. This cartridge was composed of a case formed from sheet brass that was rolled around and attached to an iron base that contained the primer. The interior of the case was lined with tissue paper. A 480-grain round-nose hardened-lead bullet, 12 parts lead and one part tin, with a paper patch around the base, was loaded into this cartridge. It created hideous internal injuries and exit wounds. On top of the powder charge was placed a glazed cardboard disc and a beeswax wad with a concave face towards the bullet. Then two more glazed cardboard discs were placed under the bullet. Cartridges for the carbine variants differed only in the weight of the bullet and the weight of the powder charge. Trials had shown that when the standard cartridge was fired in the carbine, the recoil was both painful and reduced the accuracy of the weapon. This was overcome by shortening the bullet by 0.12in, thus reducing the weight to 410 grains, and by reducing the powder charge to 70 grains of black powder.

Firing any weapon for a prolonged time leaves a greasy deposit in the chamber. However, the density of the Boxer-Henry charge, coupled with the thin cartridge, meant that there was an increased tendency, as the weapon got hotter, for it to stick to the chamber. The extractors might break or, more commonly, they would tear off the base of the cartridge and jam the breech, making it necessary to remove the debris with a cleaning rod or a knife. Combat experiences in both South Africa and Egypt demonstrated that such tearing on extraction caused difficulties and delays, particularly among inexperienced troops.

In an attempt to rectify this problem, in June 1885, a solid brass .450in cartridge case was adopted. Also in late 1885, a buckshot cartridge, containing 11 0.275in-diameter lead balls, was introduced into service. To be used in close combat, the introduction of this cartridge was a direct result of lessons learnt during the Sudanese campaigns of 1884–85 in which British troops discovered that the standard cartridge could sometimes prove to be insufficient to stop a charging warrior (Lewis 1996: 57).

Original 'Boxer' cartridge (left) and modern equivalent (right). (Courtesy of Jonathan R. Hope)

Replica pack of ten Martini-Henry cartridges. (Courtesy of Jonathan R. Hope)

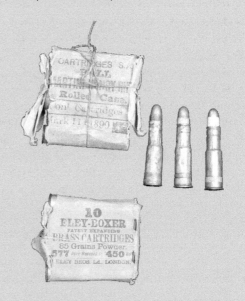

Cartridge packs and three .450in cartridges. The 480-grain round-nose bullet can be seen clearly. From left to right: blank cartridge, carbine cartridge and standard rifle cartridge. (Author)

introduction of a new rifle that 'shall be more accurate and have a flatter trajectory than the present Snider rifle' (Temple & Skennerton 1983: 23).

Clearly the Prize Competition had been a failure, given the intention of producing an acceptable breech-loading rifle for British service. There was some criticism at the time that the Trials Committee had imposed too strict a criteria, which had eliminated several promising designs at too early a stage in the trials procedure. It was felt that to be able to effectively assess the accuracy of each rifle the Trials Committee would need to lay down the barrel length, at 35in (the Snider-Enfield had a 36.5in barrel), the barrel weight, at 3lb 6oz, and the calibre, at .450in, so as to obtain a fair assessment of each entry. The cartridge to be used in the new trials was decreed to be the Government Boxer cartridge, with a bullet weight of 480 grains and powder weight of 85 grains. As the Henry rifle's breech mechanism had been considered superior in the first trial, manufacturers were instructed to fit their barrels to the Henry breech arrangements. The five firms initially invited to submit a new design were Henry, Whitworth, Westley Richards, Lancaster, Rigby and Metford, although the latter company declined to enter; all had taken part in the earlier competition (Westwood 2005: 59).

This new trial began in the spring of 1868. Tests were conducted throughout 1868 and into 1869 and, rather surprisingly, the Henry barrel showed a marked superiority in terms of accuracy and fouling over its rivals. Clearly the barrel's length, rifling and calibre had the potential to improve dramatically the accuracy of the British soldier. The Trials Committee could confidently proclaim that 'the Henry barrel, 0.45 inch bore, is that most suitable in all respects for the requirements of the service' (Temple & Skennerton 1983: 29).

With the issue of the new rifle's barrel now resolved, trials now focused on the breech mechanism. Again, rigorous tests were imposed upon a number of manufacturers' mechanisms, including those of Henry, Peabody, Martini and Remington. Rapidity of fire, and the ability to withstand mistreatment, such as sand thrown into the mechanism and exposure to the elements, were among several trials. Although the Henry mechanism again shone, it was the Martini breech mechanism which 'worked well during the trial, and when stripped the breech mechanism was in perfect order, free from rust or dust' (Temple & Skennerton 1983: 32). It now seemed clear that the Martini's failings in the earlier trials had been due to defective ammunition.

The final recommendation of the Small Arms Committee was that the rifle selected was to be a hybrid of the Martini-designed breech block and a .450in rifled barrel of seven shallow grooves designed by Henry. After the adoption of a bottle-necked rolled-brass cartridge with a bullet of 480 grains, the specifications to govern the manufacture of the new Martini-Henry rifle were issued to private contractors in February 1872.

The first pattern of the new rifle was fitted with a safety catch and stop; it had a gunmetal axis pin and keeper screw, a chequered buttplate, a wide 'V' backsight cap, a butt-mounted rear swivel, a rounded-tip cleaning rod, and an 1871 or 1872 date. It was succeeded by a second pattern, which featured an improved trigger and was dated 1872 to 1874.

Service trials continued throughout 1872 and 1873, which began to highlight various defects, mostly concerning the trigger, block axis pin, sights and striker. These issues led to even more extended trials and the manufacture of a third pattern of Martini-Henry rifle.

This third pattern, introduced as the 'Martini-Henry Rifle Mark I Approved' in July 1874, was externally similar to the ensuing Mark II rifle, but featured Mark I designation markings and 1874, 1875 or 1876 manufacture dates. Some of the third-pattern rifles may be encountered with the wide 'V' backsight cap, a butt swivel and chequered buttplate, although none was fitted with the safety catch or solid gunmetal breech-block axis pin with keeper screw on the left side of the action body. In November 1875, the final modification of the troublesome trigger mechanism, which had a tendency to discharge without warning, preceded further extensive trials, with 1,000 modified rifles sent to various regimental stations.

INTO SERVICE: PROBLEMS WITH THE MARK I

Despite the delays, the extended trials, and the inherent problems with the Mark I, the overwhelming view from the soldiers who used this new rifle was one of delight, for this single-shot weapon offered them simplicity of operation. The trigger guard was the actuating lever, which, once depressed, allowed the breech block, hinged as it was at the rear, to drop down away from the breech face. As this happened, an ejector forced the spent cartridge out of the breech. A new cartridge could then be hand-loaded into the breech. Lifting the trigger guard closed the breech and the weapon was ready to fire.

Yet faults, and complaints, with the Martini-Henry rifle continued to surface. The most frequent complaint was of undersighting,[1] although this issue was never definitively proven and was nullified in tests in which the rifle was rested on sandbags. Broken strikers and tumblers were also a common reported fault. The pull-off was also complained of as being irregular. However, it was not long before one particularly serious problem became obvious – the premature ignition of the cartridge. This was most prevalent at overseas stations, but did also occur at home. For example, in January 1875 the commanding officer of the 95th Regiment at Fleetwood, Lancashire, reported: 'I have to state that on the occasion of a portion of the regiment firing blank ammunition with the Martini-Henry rifle on closing the breech block of one of the rifles the cartridge exploded on two different occasions' (quoted in Temple & Skennerton 1983: 100). In May that year the commanding officer of the 1/4th Regiment, now stationed at Gibraltar, wrote:

> In two rifles it had been found that on closing the breech after firing, the striker had been released. Experiments had been made, and it was found that if any small substance was introduced between the outer

---

1 Undersighting occurs when the round falls short of the distance judged by the sight on the rifle. For example, the sight may be set at 500yd, but the round travels only 400yd

bearing of the trigger and the guard, the spring and striker were released on closing the breech. Two cartridges had been exploded in this way. (Quoted in Temple & Skennerton 1983: 100)

Also in May 1875, the commanding officer of the 1/Scots Fusilier Guards reported: 'A man having broken the sear spring of his Martini rifle, I find on examination that it is possible to load and fire the rifle without discovering that the sear spring is broken, and that when so loaded the slightest touch on the trigger, or a knock of the butt on the ground, will cause the rifle to go off' (Quoted in Temple & Skennerton 1983: 100).

At first the Adjutant-General[2] (AG), General Sir Richard Airey (1803–81), considered these to be isolated cases that did not require an expensive and difficult modification, but the Army continued to receive complaints. The Inspector of Munitions at the Royal Marine Artillery Barracks, Portsmouth, recounted that during the annual course of practice with the Martini-Henry, some of the rifles exploded their cartridges during the act of closing the lever. Furthermore, of the 280 rifles issued during this practice, 12 experienced either broken strikers or main springs. Thus throughout 1875–76, the AG authorized modifications to the trigger mechanisms to be implemented so as to rectify the problems with breakages and accidental discharge. Various trigger trials also took place during this period.

What was now becoming a catalogue of problems with the Martini-Henry rifle was accompanied by 'a torrent of adverse criticism' (Miller 2010: 22). The performance of the Martini-Henry rifle was even openly criticized in Parliament; Conservative MP Sir Walter Bartelott, a prominent member of the rifle-volunteer force and a friend of the gunmaker Westley Richards, tried unsuccessfully to get parliamentary inquiries into the Martini-Henry's selection, on both 28 April 1871 and 9 June 1876. Writing in the journal *Engineering*, W.P.P. Marshall went so far as to suggest that 'to adopt such a rifle would not be a mechanical credit to the country' (Marshall 1871: 22).

With further use, yet more problems began to appear. For example, the barrel was prone to overheating and undersighting of the sights for ranges in excess of 500yd was revealed. As a result of trials, a sliding sight with a height adjustment of 0.060in was adopted. It was sealed as a pattern with the Mark II rifles in April 1877 and incorporated

2 The Adjutant-General was responsible for developing the Army's personnel policies and supporting its people with equipment, accommodation and other requirements

THE MARTINI-HENRY EXPOSED

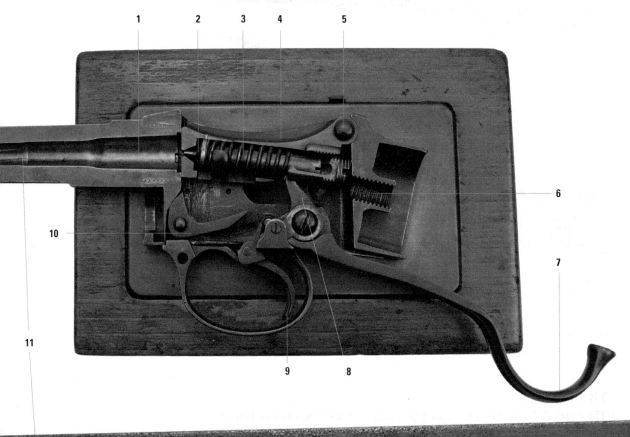

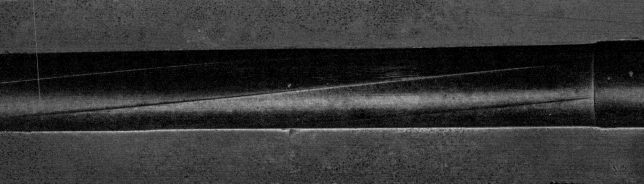

Martini-Henry Rifle Mark I, 1st Pattern

1. Chamber
2. Striker
3. Striker spring
4. Breech block
5. Breech block axis pin
6. Stock bolt thread
7. Lever
8. Tumbler
9. Trigger
10. Extractor
11. Henry rifling, with seven shallow grooves

Photos © Royal Armouries, PR.5559

The single-shot breech-loading Martini-Henry Rifle Mark II. This example was adapted from a Mark I. (Courtesy of Jonathan R. Hope)

a previously approved 'V'-notch. The deepened notch was also applied to the sight cap, and then became the standard form for all subsequent Martini-Henry rifles, until the introduction of the Lewes sights on the Mark V and Mark VI.

THE MARK II

The Mark II, by far the most widely produced mark of the Martini-Henry rifle, was approved for service on 25 April 1877. Comparing the third-pattern Mark I with the Mark II externally, the latter had no butt swivel; a smooth butt plate; a different trigger unit; a different cleaning rod; a trigger guard with rounded edges at rear; and a back sight with deeper notches, to improve the line of sight. The complete trigger assembly, breech block and extractor were significantly different in the Mk II, as the relevant pattern-book entry stated:

> The alterations in the action are as follows –
> The tumbler is of a new pattern, acting directly on the trigger, the tumbler rest and screw have been abolished.
> The trigger is of a new pattern.
> The trigger guard has a shield covering the trigger knuckle.
> The block has a slot cut through the underside to allow for the play of the tumbler. The extractor has the sides of its lower arm parallel throughout. (Quoted in Temple & Skennerton 1983: 116)

All these modifications were designed to obtain a more regular pull-off of the trigger, and to stop the rifle's liability to accidentally discharge, caused by dirt becoming deposited between the trigger and the trigger guard of the action.

The garrison at Fort Commeline, Pretoria, 1881, with Martini-Henry Rifles Mark II. (Courtesy of Ian Knight)

By the time the Mark II was approved for service – it entered production in 1878 – a total of 314,633 Mark I rifles, of all three patterns, had been manufactured between 1873 and 1877, and some had been issued to colonial governments. These latter weapons were not modified for some years, if at all, and have become great collector's items. The remaining rifles were modified to become Mark IIs throughout 1877–79, with the result that few original Mark II rifles were produced in these years. For example, in 1879 45,600 Mark II rifles were produced, but in 1880 only 33 were. This low figure was caused by the adoption of the Martini-Henry Rifle Mark III on 22 August 1879, resulting in the cutback of Mark II production at the Royal Small Arms Factory (RSAF) Enfield. The Mark II was, however, carried on in production by the trade, as this of course obviated any great alteration in their machinery, which a changeover to the Mark III would have required. Thus 6,000 Mark IIs were supplied in 1880, and contracts for Mark II rifles were given to Birmingham Small Arms (BSA) Co. in 1886 (10,500) and 1887 (53,100). These were produced at a rate of 400 per week, and the last delivery under these contracts was made in June 1890.

Martini-Henry rifles

	Overall length	Barrel length	Overall weight	Barrel weight
Mark I	49.0in	33.20in	8lb 12oz	3lb 6oz
Mark II (long butt)	49.5in	33.19in	8lb 10.5oz	3lb 6oz
Mark II (short butt)	49.0in	33.19in	8lb 8oz	3lb 6oz
Mark III	49.5in	33.20in	9lb	3lb 6oz
Mark IV	49.5in	33.20in	9lb 1oz	3lb 6oz

THE MARTINI-HENRY CAVALRY AND ARTILLERY CARBINES

By early 1871 the first Service pattern of the Martini-Henry rifle was beginning to be introduced and work began that year to produce carbine variants. By June 1871 the RSAF submitted one specimen each of artillery and cavalry carbines, with a sword bayonet for the former. The artillery carbine had the same muzzle diameter as the rifle, so it could mount the rifle's Pattern 1860 Sword Bayonet. The cavalry carbine and the artillery carbine were each made to the length of the corresponding Snider-Enfield carbine – i.e. 36.75in for the cavalry and 40in for the artillery. These weapons were sent to the Hythe range in Kent for trials against the equivalent Snider-Enfield carbine models at ranges of 300yd and 500yd. The new carbines were found to be more accurate at 300yd but worse at 500yd. Furthermore, the recoil of the new weapons was found to be excessive and the barrels heated so rapidly that grip was interfered with. It was decided in early 1873 that in their current form, the carbines could not be adopted because of their excessive recoil. Work began on a method to reduce this.

In October 1873 RSAF Enfield reported that in order to cut the recoil of the Martini-Henry carbine there seemed to be no alternative but to lessen the charge of the cartridge, either by reducing the weight of powder and retaining the same bullet, or by reducing both the powder and the bullet weight. As the latter option would require a different calibre for the new carbine, this was rejected, and if the issue of recoil could not be solved then for practical and financial reasons the Snider carbine would have remained in service. Experiments were continued with the Martini-Henry carbines, using the existing chamber and cartridge case, but with a reduced charge. The advantage claimed for this arrangement was that in emergencies the carbines could use rifle ammunition and vice versa. Carbines sighted for a 70/380-grain cartridge were produced in the fourth and fifth trial patterns. The 19th Hussars, stationed in Hythe, Kent, were asked to conduct trials with the new cavalry carbine with the reduced

Scottish Yeomanry trooper with a Martini-Henry Cavalry Carbine Mark I. (Author, from Greener's *The Gun and its Development*, 1881)

ABOVE LEFT Two Indian Army soldiers on foot, and a mounted lancer. The sowar (cavalryman) is armed with a lance and a carbine. One of the infantry soldiers is armed with a Martini-Henry rifle. They stand outside a Moghul-style building in Quetta, June 1897. (National Army Museum)

ABOVE RIGHT A late-Victorian artilleryman, armed with a Martini-Henry Artillery Carbine Mark I with Pattern 1879 Sawback Bayonet, Bombay, 1900. (Courtesy of Edward Garcia, Soldiers of the Queen website)

powder cartridge and in August 1874 the commanding officer of the 19th Hussars was able to report that the accuracy was satisfactory, and recoil very slight (Temple & Skennerton: 1983 120).

The sixth trial pattern of the cavalry carbine was prepared in early 1876 with new action components from the Mark II rifle's trigger mechanism; the first Service pattern of the cavalry carbine was approved in September 1877 and was ordered into immediate production. A staggering 25,000 were produced by the end of 1878, demonstrating the capacity of RSAF Enfield to produce a large number of weapons quickly. A second Service pattern of the Cavalry Carbine Mark I, with a leather rear-sight cover for added protection, was approved. These modifications were added to the sealed pattern and fitted to all subsequent arms. A total of 74,895 cavalry carbines were made between 1878 and 1889, including two orders for the Indian Government – 5,000 in 1886 and a further 4,100 in 1888 (Temple & Skennerton 1995: 628).

The artillery carbine was accepted into service in April 1878. With the need for this variant to mount a bayonet it differed from the cavalry carbine in that 'the nose cap is altered in form and size to take an upper band with bar, for the sword bayonet; the front edge of the bar is rounded off to prevent injury to the hand when the arm is held at the "order". The carbine is fitted with swivels for a sling' (Temple & Skennerton 1995: 628). Between 1879 and 1894, 59,919 carbines of this variant were made, with over 58,000 produced at RSAF Enfield.

The Martini-Henry Artillery Carbine Mark II appeared in 1892. This was a converted arm made by reducing the length of the Martini-Henry Rifle Mark II to that of the standard carbine. The Mark II artillery carbine was intended for issue only to Garrison Artillery, but was later supplied to school cadet and other Volunteer forces. In the period 1892–96, 38,407 were produced, all at the Enfield works (Temple & Skennerton 1995: 629).

Martini-Henry carbines

	Overall length	Barrel length	Overall weight	Barrel weight
Cavalry Carbine Mark I	37.6in	21.35in	7lb 8oz	2lb 1.75oz
Artillery Carbine Mark I	37.6in	21.35in	7lb 12oz	2lb 4.75oz
Artillery Carbine Mark II	37.6in	21.35in	7lb 9oz	2lb 4.75oz
Artillery Carbine Mark III	37.6in	21.35in	7lb 6oz	2lb 4.75oz

THE MARTINI-HENRY RIFLE MARK III

The Martini-Henry Rifle Mark III was a logical follow-on from the cavalry and artillery carbines, using the improved action mechanism, and the forend hook as introduced with the carbine. It also incorporated some modifications to the rear sights, but its general appearance was similar to the Mark II. The new pattern was approved on 22 August 1879 and was initially considered as a lower-cost arm for the militia, with the Mark II remaining the front-line weapon. Between 1880 and 1890, 232,320 Mark IIIs were produced. They differed from the Mark II in the following particulars:

Backsight: bed – altered with an inclination so as to correct the permanent deflection due to the rifling.
Barrel: has a double lump at the breech end, one projection on the upper and one on the under surface, as in the case of Martini-Henry carbines. This allows a better bearing to be obtained when the barrel is 'breeched up' to the body, and gives additional strength to the chamber.
Block: wider at the front to make it steadier when firing, and is the same as that for the Martini-Henry carbines.

A Martini-Henry Artillery Carbine Mark I, with a Pattern 1859 Cutlass Bayonet that has had a 9.25in saw added on the upper blade. (Author)

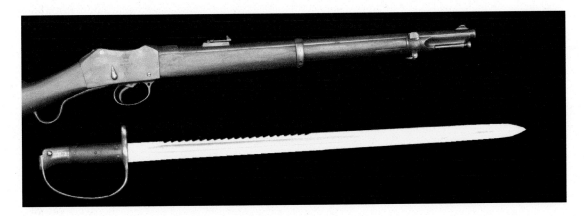

Striker: the diameter of the collar is increased to make it a sliding fit in the spring chamber of the block – same as the carbines. (Quoted in Temple & Skennerton 1983: 142)

THE MARTINI-HENRY RIFLE MARK IV

According to Dennis Lewis, the Martini-Henry Rifle Mark IV, approved for service in 1887, was the .450in rifle that 'should never have been' (Lewis 1996: 26). With other nations moving towards the adoption of new small-bore repeating arms, the British also began to look at producing such a weapon. The Mark IV or 'hump-back' long-lever Martini-Henry rifle was produced in the short hiatus before the introduction of the .303in magazine rifle. The most notable difference from the Mark III was the new weapon's cut-down rear portion of the receiver, stepped down immediately behind the breech-block axis pin to form a more comfortable grip.

A comparison between Martini-Henry Rifles Mark II (above) and Mark III (below). Note the variation in the attachment of the forend, and the difference in the size of the block mechanism. (Courtesy of Alan M. Petrillo)

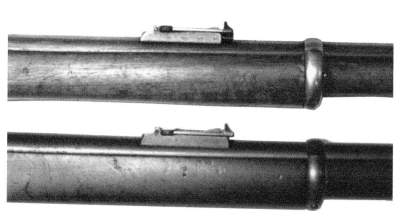

Another comparison between the Martini-Henry Rifles Mark II (above) and Mark III (below). Note the difference in how the forends have been attached. The Mark III offers slightly better protection of the user's grip from a hot barrel. (Courtesy of Alan M. Petrillo)

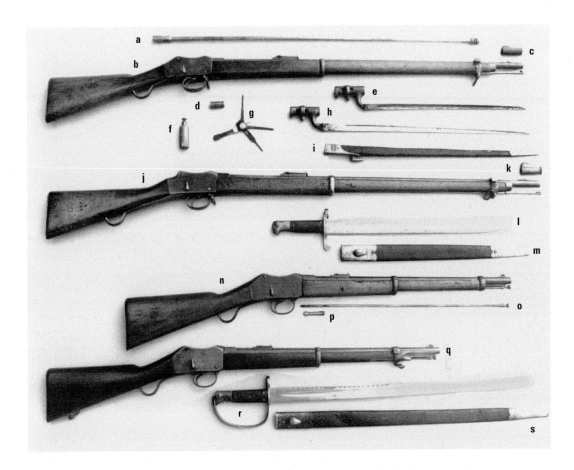

The breech block also differed; the Mark IV's body was narrowed and the angle on the underside changed so as to clear a newly designed extractor, which was 0.5in longer and had a slot in the lower arm to clear the trigger. This new extractor, along with the 3in-longer operating lever, had been designed to improve the extraction of fired cases. Between 1888 and 1890 100,001 Mark IVs were made, all at RSAF Enfield (Temple & Skennerton 1995: 628). The majority of these weapons were supplied to the Indian Army, as new .303in calibre variants rapidly made the Mark IV obsolete for front-line British Army regiments.

TRADE-PATTERN MARTINI-HENRYS

As well as Service weapons, Trade-pattern Martini-Henry rifles and carbines were also produced. Many of these arms were made by one or another of the private companies supplying Martinis to the British Government, as the patterns, jigs, tools and so on were readily available, provided of course that suitable arrangements were made for the payment of royalties to the holders of the Martini and Henry patents. When the private factories were not fully utilized with British Government orders, the production of weapons for other countries was one way to keep the factories in operation. Such privately made weapons were frequently used

FROM TOP:
(a) .297/230 Morris tube (used to enable the rifle to fire a smaller-calibre round) for the Martini-Henry rifle;
(b) Martini-Henry Rifle Mark III, with (c) brass nose cap;
(d) snap cap; (e) Pattern 1853 Bushed Socket Bayonet;
(f) oil bottle;
(g) jag key implement tool;
(h) Pattern 1876 Socket Bayonet, with (i) scabbard; (j) Martini-Henry Rifle Mark IV, with (k) brass nose cap;
(l) Pattern 1887 Sword Bayonet, with (m) scabbard;
(n) Martini-Henry Cavalry Carbine Mark I, with (o) extra cleaning rod and (p) jag; (q) Martini-Henry Artillery Carbine Mark I;
(r) Pattern 1879 Sawback Bayonet, with (s) scabbard. (Courtesy of Ian Skennerton)

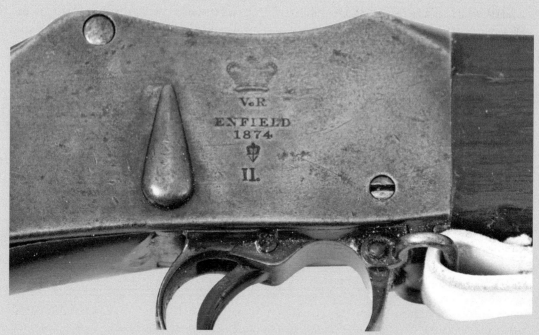

The marking of a Martini-Henry Rifle Mark I, which has been converted to a Mark II variant. (Courtesy of Jonathan R. Hope)

Manufacturers and markings

Although there were subtle differences between some of the action markings on the various types of Service Martini-Henrys, the markings pertaining were typical on all patterns. In this order (normally top to bottom), the markings indicated: the Sovereign's cypher; the manufacturer's code (1–5); the year of manufacture; and the lock viewer's mark. The Martini-Henry Service rifles and carbines were produced in just five arms factories across Britain. An examination of lock viewer's marks and the manufacturer's code, which can be found engraved upon the body of the action, as well as roundels imprinted on the stock, readily identified both where and when each weapon was made. The arms factories were recorded thus:

1. BSA & Co.: Birmingham Small Arms and Metal Company.

BSA began in June 1861 in the Gun Quarter, Birmingham; it was founded specifically to manufacture guns by machinery. It was formed by a group of 14 gunsmith members of the Birmingham Small Arms Trade Association. The market had moved against British gunsmiths following the outbreak of the Crimean War in 1854 because the Board of Ordnance's Royal Small Arms Factory at Enfield had introduced new American-made machinery, and Enfield's greatly increased output had been achieved with reduced reliance on skilled craftsmen. The War Office provided this new grouping of gunsmiths free access to technical drawings and their facilities at their Enfield factory.

BODY DESIGNATION MARKINGS—
e.g.

B.S.A.& M.Co.
1876
II
Martini-Henry Rifle Mk II

ENFIELD
1879
I.C.1
Martini-Henry Cavalry or Artillery Carbine

ENFIELD
1886
I.V.
Martini-Henry Rifle Mk IV

ENFIELD
1886
I
Enfield-Martini Rifle Mk I

B.S.A.& M.Co.
1889
I
Martini-Metford Rifle Mk II, ex- VI

H.R.B.Co.
1892
M.M. .303
I*
Martini-Metford Cavalry Carbine Mk I*

ENFIELD
1896
I
Martini-Enfield Rifle Mk I

ENFIELD
1899
M.E. .303
A.C. III
Martini-Enfield Artillery Carbine Mk III

1. The Sovereign's (or Royal) Cypher
2. Manufacturer's code
3. Year of manufacture
4. Lock viewer's mark.

V.R
ENFIELD — 2
1876 — 3
— 4
— 1

Fig. 1 – Typical Action Body Markings.

2. Enfield: Royal Small Arms Factory (RSAF), Enfield Lock, Middlesex. By 1861 this was the main government factory and by the 1870s was producing 2,000 rifles and carbines weekly. It became the principal factory for the mass production of both Martini-Henry rifles and carbines. Enfield also supervised the manufacture of Service Martinis by private companies by producing the pattern arms and drawings for these weapons, and appointing the inspectors who viewed and tested them.

3. HRB Co.: Henry Rifled Barrel, Engineering and Small Arms Company, Eagle Wharf, Hoxton, East London. This factory was involved by the late 1880s with the conversion of Martini-Henry arms into Martini-Metford patterns, followed in the mid-1890s by the manufacture of Martini-Henry rifles and carbines to government contracts, often for the Indian Government.

4. LSA Co.: London Small Arms Company Ltd, Old Ford Road, Bow, East London. LSA was originally wholly privately owned and operated, and was not a large factory. To ensure survival the firm entered into an agreement with BSA & Co. in 1867 such that all contracts for arms won by either factory would be shared in the proportion of 40 per cent for LSA and 60 per cent for BSA. This arrangement held good until 1878, when NA & A Co. Ltd negotiated an entry into the agreement; contracts were then shared in the proportions of 40 per cent for BSA, 33 per cent for NA & A and 27 per cent for LSA.

5. NA & A Co. Ltd: National Arms and Ammunition Company Ltd, Sparkbrook, Birmingham. This company had acquired the rights to the Martini patents and anticipated large government orders for Service Martinis, but it was not until the company negotiated the agreement with BSA and LSA in 1878 that any government contracts were forthcoming. It then shared contracts for the rifle from 1880 to 1883, but these were not enough to keep the company viable, and it collapsed in 1885. At a sale of its assets in 1886, the British Government purchased the entire Sparkbrook factory and it became the RSAF Birmingham Repair.

The year of manufacture indicated the calendar year in which the arm was made, rather than the financial or working year during which it was ordered. The lock viewer's mark was originally applied to the locks of muzzle-loading arms, usually those made by subcontractors who specialized in the unit, and were subsequently assembled into complete arms at the government factories. In such circumstances, the mark signified that the locks had been examined for functionality, conformity and pattern. The official carrying out this inspection was known as the 'lock viewer', hence the term 'lock viewer's mark'. It seems to have fulfilled a similar purpose with Service Martini-Henrys, but as the weapon was generally made in one location, with little subcontracting, it would seem that the lock viewer's mark was more convention than necessity. Eventually, it was deemed superfluous and was abolished in 1897, so it is not noted on weapons dated after this year.

The mark of the weapon was also recorded on the body action, always in Roman numerals. Hence, 'II' indicated a Mark II variant. The year of manufacture, combined with the mark number, could be used to identify whether the weapon had been modified from an earlier variant. Thus, the year of '1874' with a mark number of 'II' would indicate that the weapon had once been a Mark I, but had been improved and modified some time between 1877 and 1879. In addition, on a carbine, the letters 'A.C.' or 'C.C.' defined whether the weapon was an artillery or cavalry carbine.

The roundel markings found on the butt of both rifle and carbine also indicate the manufacturer and the mark, although there appears to be less conformity between the manufacturers in the style and detail of the roundel. It is often the case that the information codes on the roundels do not agree with that on the body action; in such cases the latter should be considered the more accurate of the two. The exact meaning of many of the roundel codes has been lost and thus any attempted translation would be little more than speculation.

BODY STAMPS & MARKINGS—
e.g.

	Royal cypher Victoria Regina
ENFIELD	Maker
1880	Year of manufacture
⚘	Lock viewer's mark
III	Mark designation
1	Class mark

1   2   3   4   5

Fig.4 – Lock Viewer's Marks –
1. BSA Co.
2. Enfield
3. HRB Co.
4. LSA Co.
5. NA & A Co.

(Markings courtesy of Ian Skennerton)

A Trade-pattern Martini-Henry Rifle Mark II. (Courtesy of Ian Skennerton)

by home and colonial Volunteers, Militia and rifle clubs. With their similarity to the Service arms, such weapons are often referred to as 'Volunteer patterns'.

The Trade patterns appeared alongside the early development of the Martini-Henry and were improved in parallel with most subsequent Service patterns up to the Martini-Enfield era. One company particularly active in the production of Trade patterns was the Braendlin Armoury Company of London and Birmingham, although others were made at the BSA, LSA and NA & A factories. As well as the manufacturer's mark, such rifles can also be found bearing the name of individual retailers, such as 'Army and Navy' and 'Alex. Fraser Barnett' (Lewis 1996: 53). While Trade models frequently corresponded to Service weapons, because the same tools and production processes were used, it is possible to find later marks incorporated with secondary items from earlier marks, such as cleaning rods.

Some unusual Trade arms were produced. For example, a second-pattern Martini-Henry Rifle Mark I was made in the USA for the Turkish Government in the early 1870s. The British factories were operating at full capacity to meet British Government orders, so the Turks placed the contract for manufacture in America. These arms can be identified by markings on the left side of the action body:

PEABODY & MARTINI PATENTS
MAN'F'D BY PROVIDENCE TOOL CO.
PROV. R.I. U.S.A.

In addition, companies such as Providence Tool Company of Rhode Island manufactured sporting and target rifles, based firmly on the Martini-Henry rifle, for the civilian market. In Britain, while some of these civilian arms were no more than Service pattern arms with commercial markings, other Martini-Henry variants represented the top end of the most prestigious gunmakers' output. Thus sporting and target arms were produced by the likes of Westley Richards, S.W. Silver & Co. and W.J. Jeffrey & Co. Such rifles, because of their almost legendary 'stopping-power', became the weapons of choice for big-game-hunting gentlemen from the 1880s to the early 1900s. Some of these interesting arms were frequently engraved with African or Indian animals, such as elephants or tigers, and possessed fine-quality French walnut stocks.

Trade-pattern Martini-Henrys made a final appearance in the early years of World War I as a special emergency supply of arms for training the large numbers of volunteers for the British Army. With .303in magazine rifles urgently required at the front line, the Martini arms were found to be quicker and cheaper to make. They did not have to conform to a specific pattern, but only had to chamber the Service cartridge, so as to remove logistical problems, and to conform to standard proof tests for safety reasons. The result was a varied collection of Martini arms ranging from rifles to carbines. Once the initial emergency had been met, these non-standard weapons were gradually withdrawn and relegated to use by non-combatants, where they obtained the official name of 'Home Guard Pattern'.

The various marks and patterns of Martini-Henry rifles and carbines, with their variety of cartridges and bayonets, became the iconic weapons of the British Empire throughout the 1880s. However, just as the Snider was to be viewed as a stop-gap weapon, the .450in Martini-Henry was to have a short service life in the British Army. Its immediate successors, the Martini-Metford and Martini-Enfield, similar in design but of smaller calibre, were also to serve for only a few years, such was the pace of military technological development at the end of the 19th century.

MARTINI-METFORD AND MARTINI-ENFIELD RIFLES AND CARBINES

The acceptance into British service, in late 1888, of the .303in Lee-Metford Magazine Rifle marked the demise of the Martini-Henry rifle in front-line use, but not the end of development of the weapon. It was decided that the Martini-Henry should also be produced in .303in calibre so as to obviate ammunition-supply problems. To that end, a series of arms consisting of conversions of basic Martini-Henry patterns was planned and these conversions were initially to consist of re-barrelled Martini-Henry Rifles Mark II and Mark III, and the Martini-Henry Cavalry Carbine Mark I. The new .303in barrels were to be rifled on the Metford system as used in the magazine rifle. The re-barrelled Mark III was designated the Martini-

A Martini-Metford Artillery Carbine Mark II, converted from a Martini-Henry Rifle Mark II. (Courtesy of Ian Skennerton)

CARBINE (ARTILLERY) M.H. 0·45 MARK II (CONVERTED FROM RIFLE M.H.MARK II.)
FULL SIZE

A.I.D
4

The very rare .303 Mark V
Martini-Henry. Only six were ever
made, of which two are in the
collections of the Royal
Armouries, Leeds. (© Royal
Armouries, XII.3321)

Henry Rifle Mark V; the re-barrelled Mark II was designated the Martini-Henry Rifle Mark VI; and the re-barrelled cavalry carbine was designated the Martini-Henry Cavalry Carbine Mark II.

The Martini-Henry Rifle Mark V

This mark was to be produced by converting the Martini-Henry Rifle Mark III; the conversion included the fitting of a new barrel and breech block, with related items. The barrel, and the forend and its furniture, were patterned on those of the Lee-Metford, so that arm's Pattern 1888 Sword Bayonet (23.75in long, with a blade length of 18.5in) was to be used. Another feature of the new magazine rifle used by the Martini-Henry Rifle Mark V was the Lewes sighting system, which was copied from the French 8mm Modèle 1886 Lebel rifle and consisted of a square-notch rear sight, and a square-topped foresight, cut with a narrow groove. The backsight was graduated to 1,900yd. Temple and Skennerton believe only six Mark IIIs were fitted with .303in barrels 'and, for lack of evidence to the contrary, were probably the only arms of the type to be made' (Temple & Skennerton 1983: 153).

The Martini-Henry Rifle Mark VI

Like the Mark V, the Martini-Henry Rifle Mark VI was intended to be converted from an older Martini-Henry mark, but the Mark VI was to retain an appearance similar to the original Martini-Henry arm. The proliferation of Martini-Henry Mark IIs still in circulation, or in store, meant that it was this mark that was most commonly converted into the Mark VI. The resemblance to the original Martini-Henry was achieved by making the new .303in barrel to the same profile as the Henry barrel and utilizing most of the original furniture. The Mark VI thus mounted the standard Martini-Henry rifle sword bayonets, but could not use the Pattern 1853 or Pattern 1876 socket bayonets because of the form of the foresight block. The sights were the Lewes pattern. In its original form the Mark VI was intended as a conversion of existing arms, but, as it was found that there was still a demand from the colonies for new Martini-Henry Mark IIs, at the time of its inception, the Mark VI was subsequently produced as a new arm in its own right, using Mark II components where possible. This led to the mark being approved as a new weapon.

Manufacture of the Mark VI began without delay. All Mark VIs were manufactured by BSA & Co. to an order for 9,600 arms. As the company was not set up to produce .303in barrels, arrangements were made for RSAF Enfield to supply 3,000 barrels. The Mark VI was issued mainly to the colonies, and, for all the haste to get it into production, about half of

the weapons made were still in store in 1892. The likely reason was that the Lewes sight[3] was found to be very unsatisfactory, being nearly 300yd undersighted at 500yd range. Indeed the sighting of all .303in British Service arms reverted to the standard barleycorn foresight and 'V'-notch backsight after the Lewes sights were officially abolished in early 1892. The sights on the Mark VI were likewise altered and the variant was finally issued.

.303in Martini-Metford Rifle Mark I (S.A. Pattern) with Pattern 1888 Sword Bayonet and scabbard. (Courtesy of Ian Skennerton)

Martini-Metford carbines				
	Overall length	Barrel length	Overall weight	Barrel weight
Cavalry Carbine Mark I	37.6in	21.3in	8lb 4oz	2lb 1.75oz
Cavalry Carbine Mark II	37.6in	21.3in	8lb 3oz	2lb 1.70oz
Cavalry Carbine Mark III	37.6in	21.3in	6lb 11oz	2lb 1.5oz
Artillery Carbine Mark I	37.5in	21.3in	7lb 11oz	2lb 4.75oz
Artillery Carbine Mark II	36.8in	21.0in	6lb 13.5oz	2lb 4.75oz
Artillery Carbine Mark III	37.3in	21.0in	7lb 6oz	2lb 4.75oz

The Martini-Henry Cavalry Carbine Mark II

The development of the .303in Martini-Henry Cavalry Carbine Mark II started in July 1889 when the Commander-in-Chief, Prince George, the Duke of Cambridge (1819–1904), decided that, as a result of the adoption of the Lee-Metford Magazine Rifle for the infantry, it was essential that the cavalry and the horse and field artillery should be able to use a common cartridge. As it seemed there was no probability of a suitable magazine carbine being developed in the near future, it was decided that, in the interim, patterns of single-loading carbines for both cavalry and artillery should be produced. The Mark II was a simple conversion of the Mark I, which consisted mainly of replacing the barrel with one of .303in calibre but of the same profile, so that the original forend and furniture could be used with the minimum of alteration. In keeping with the rifles, the carbines were fitted

3 The Lewes is a 'V' notch cut into a raised platform on the foresight block; the conventional block is an inverted 'V' or 'barleycorn' on top of the block. To describe simply, the Lewes aimed by looking down a groove, while the normal sight aimed with the use of the top of a point

with the troublesome Lewes sights. The Martini-Henry Cavalry Carbine Mark II was the only .303in carbine to be actually named and produced as a Martini-Henry. It was approved in May 1891, but only kept its name until August of that year, for the Martini-Henry Rifle Marks V and VI – as well as the Martini-Henry Cavalry Carbine Mark II – were soon to disappear.

In August 1891 it was decided that the converted Martini-Henry arms using the Metford rifling and barrel would require a change of nomenclature. The Martini-Henry Rifle Mark V became the Martini-Metford Rifle Mark I; the Martini-Henry Rifle Mark VI became the Martini-Metford Rifle Mark II; and the Martini-Henry Cavalry Carbine Mark II became the Martini-Metford Cavalry Carbine Mark I.

By strict definition, and with the Henry barrel no longer in use, the Martini-Henry rifle was now no longer in front-line use with Regular British troops, although these weapons looked very similar to the Martini-Henry arms they replaced. Because of the availability of the magazine rifle for the Regular infantry, the newly named Martini-Metford rifles as a group were not considered front-line Service weapons, and their subsequent employment was confined mostly to colonial and Militia units. The carbines, on the other hand, because of the initial lack of a magazine carbine, were issued to the Regular forces using carbines, and so enjoyed full Service status.

After a few years of using the .303in cordite cartridge with the Metford barrel it was found that the hotter gases from the combustion of the cordite charge, as compared to the black powder, caused severe erosion at the breech end of the barrel. This erosion in some instances reduced the

.303in Martini-Metford Cavalry Carbine patterns. From top: three examples of the Martini-Metford Cavalry Carbine Mark I (this mark was converted from the Martini-Henry Cavalry Carbines Mark I and Mark II); a Martini-Metford Cavalry Carbine Mark II, converted from the Martini-Henry Artillery Carbine Mark I; and a Martini-Metford Cavalry Carbine Mark III, converted from the Martini-Henry Rifle Mark II. Four of the five weapons are accompanied by protective nose caps. (Courtesy of Ian Skennerton)

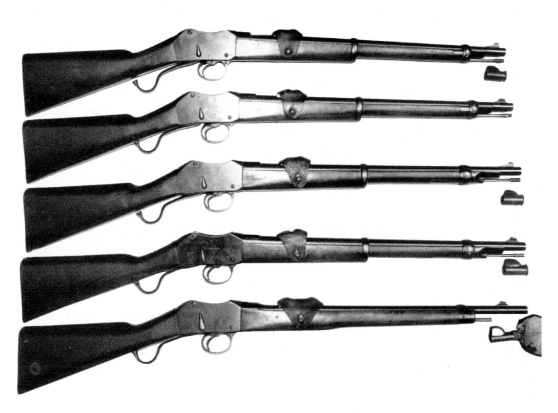

expected life of the bore by 50 per cent or more. To obviate this problem a new form of rifling was developed at RSAF Enfield, and after extensive trials had shown that it resisted the effects of the cordite combustion to a greater degree than the Metford rifling, it was approved for service in 1895. The new rifling was quickly incorporated into the Service arms, with the term 'Enfield' being substituted for 'Metford' in the nomenclature of all new patterns using this form of barrel. The resultant series of Martini arms thus became Martini-Enfield rifles or carbines.

Martini-Enfield rifles and carbines

The Martini-Enfield rifles varied in detail from the previous Martini-Metford rifles, but there was a certain resemblance between them and the Martini-Metford Rifle Mark II. The Martini-Enfield carbines, however, were practically identical to the Martini-Metford carbines; the main differences between them were minor changes in the sighting, and the rifling of the barrel. The Martini-Enfield rifles were all converted from Martini-Henry rifles, and were fitted with a new barrel, lighter and shorter than the original (to conform to magazine-rifle length and profile), and a wooden hand guard of the magazine-rifle type was also fitted to the top rear of the barrel between the action body and the rear sight. There was no provision left for a sword bayonet, as only a socket bayonet was intended to be used. The foresight block was made similar to that of the Martini-Henry rifle for this reason. Like the Martini-Metford rifles, the Martini-Enfield rifles were not British Service issue, so they too were

.303in Martini-Metford Artillery Carbine patterns. From top: Martini-Metford Artillery Carbine Mark I, converted from the Martini-Henry Artillery Carbine Mark I; Martini-Metford Artillery Carbine Mark II, converted from the Martini-Henry Rifle Mark II; two examples of the Martini-Metford Artillery Carbine Mark III, the lower one with cleaning rod. The second group of Martini-Metford Carbines (Cavalry Mark III and Artillery Mark II and Mark III) were made to an entirely new pattern, which necessitated a new shortened barrel and forend (with nose cap only) and no upper or lower bands. The sighting was also different, as these carbines had a rear sight the same size as that on the rifle, and the leaf was graduated for cordite to 2,000yd. With these sights the top action of the body in front of the block had to be filed down to enable the sights to be seen when the leaf was lowered onto the bed. (Courtesy of Ian Skennerton)

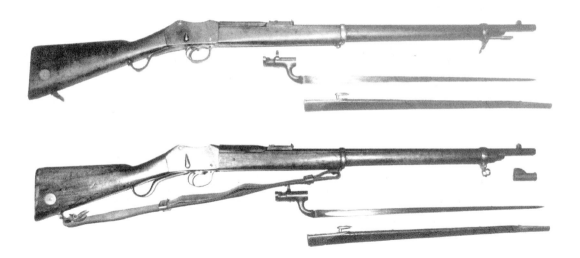

Martini-Enfield Rifles Mark I (above) and Mark II (below), each with Pattern 1895 Socket Bayonet and scabbard; the Mark II is accompanied by a protective nose cap. (Courtesy of Ian Skennerton)

issued mainly to the colonies and Militia units. The Martini-Enfield Rifle Mark I was produced by converting the Martini-Henry Rifle Mark III. In total 48,610 rifles were converted at RSAF Enfield during the period 1896–1903. Of these, 20,000 were purchased by the Indian Government.

The Martini-Enfield Cavalry Carbine Mark I was a conversion of the Martini-Henry Cavalry Carbine Mark I, which consisted generally of fitting the carbines with new barrels of .303in calibre with Enfield rifling. The Martini-Enfield Artillery Carbine Mark I was similarly a conversion, but this time of the Martini-Henry Rifle Mark III. It first appeared in Enfield production figures in 1897 when 3,801 were produced. Total Enfield production was in excess of 30,000 units, while the HRB Co. was given an order for 14,000 conversions. Many of these weapons were supplied to cadet and Volunteer units. The Martini-Enfield Artillery Carbine Mark II was converted from the Martini-Henry Artillery Carbine Mark I, with a total of 26,185 produced both at Enfield and HRB Co. Finally, the Martini-Enfield Artillery Carbine Mark III was converted from the Martini-Henry Rifle Mark II. Over 32,000 units of this arm were produced up until 1904.

Men of the 'Pretoria Horse' during the siege of Pretoria by the Boers in 1881. Those troopers wearing makeshift irregular British uniforms are armed with Martini-Henry rifles, while those in civilian dress hold the Westley-Richards rifle, a popular civilian weapon in the Transvaal at that time. (Courtesy of Ian Knight)

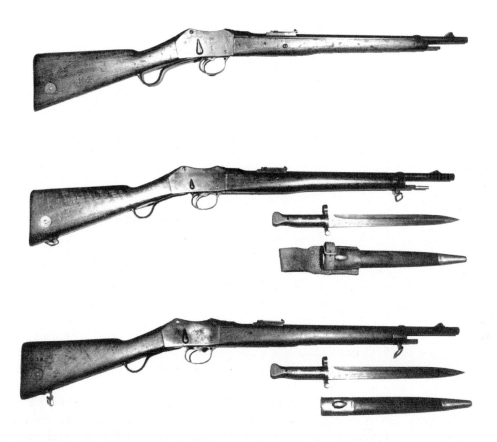

Martini-Enfield rifles and carbines				
	Overall length	**Barrel length**	**Overall weight**	**Barrel weight**
Rifle Mark I	49.5in	33.20in	9lb 12oz	3lb 8oz
Rifle Mark II	49.5in	33.20in	9lb 9oz	3lb 8oz
Cavalry Carbine Mark I	37.5in	21.3in	7lb 8oz	2lb 1.75oz
Artillery Carbine Mark I	37.3in	21.0in	7lb 3oz	2lb 4.75oz
Artillery Carbine Mark II	37.4in	21.0in	7lb 1.5oz	2lb 4.75oz
Artillery Carbine Mark III	37.3in	21.0in	7lb 0oz	2lb 4.75oz

From top: Martini-Enfield Cavalry Carbine Mark I; Martini-Enfield Artillery Carbine Mark I; Martini-Enfield Artillery Carbine Mark III. Each of the two artillery carbines is accompanied by a Pattern 1888 Sword Bayonet and scabbard; the upper scabbard has its belt attachment. (Courtesy of Ian Skennerton)

These very significant quantities of both Martini-Enfield rifles and carbines that were produced into the early years of the 19th century serve to illustrate the high demand for these weapons from the colonies, as well as Volunteer units in Britain. These figures also indicate that in the late 1890s the British Government struggled to produce the .303in magazine rifle in sufficient quantities to meet the worldwide demand for such weapons.

USE

The rifle of an expansionist decade

THE 9th CAPE FRONTIER WAR

Although the Martini-Henry was first fired in anger during the Perak Campaign of 1875–76 (in what is now Malaysia) by such regiments as the 80th (Staffs) and 3rd (Buffs), it was not until 1878 that the rifle saw extensive front-line service, both in the Eastern Cape, South Africa, and later that year in Afghanistan. At the battle of Nyumaga on 12 January 1878, during the 9th Cape Frontier War, the new rifle proved its worth. The British commander, Sir Arthur Cunynghame, was very impressed by the performance of the Martini-Henry in the hands of British Regulars of the 1/24th Regiment, and wrote, 'At no time had the power of the Martini Henry been more conspicuously shown; indeed, it was perhaps the first occasion when it had been fairly used by the British army' (Knight & Castle 2004: 26). It should be noted that the Martini-Henry Cavalry Carbine Mark I did not enter service until December 1878, and did not reach the front line in Zululand until March 1879. Troopers of the Frontier Light Horse would have either used the Snider-Enfield Carbine or the .577in/.450in Swinburne-Henry Carbine; the latter resembled the Martini-Henry Cavalry Carbine Mark I, but it had internal workings that were completely different and was more liable to jamming than the Martini. The main design difference offered by the Swinburne-Henry was that it was cocked via a large thumb-piece on the cocking indicator, not the under-lever like the Martini-Henry. This was a huge advantage over the Martini-Henry Cavalry Carbine Mark I, in that troopers could safely stow the Swinburne-Henry loaded in its leather saddle sling.

Cunynghame and his troops were again to be thankful for the devastating stopping-power of the Martini-Henry at the battle of Centane on 7 February 1878, when 450 British troops, armed with the new rifle, defeated 4,000 Gcaleka warriors under the command of the rebellious chief, Sandile. Supported by native allies, the Mfengu, and locally recruited men of the Frontier Light Horse (FLH), the troops of the 1/24th Regiment awaited the onslaught of the Gcaleka from concealed trenches. At a range of 900yd the muzzle-loaders of the Mfengu and the carbines of the FLH opened fire upon the charging mass. It quickly became apparent that these weapons lacked the stopping-power to thwart the advancing warriors and if anything the fire seemed to spur them on.

As the advance reached a watercourse at the foot of the British position, the helmets of the 1/24th Regiment appeared atop the hidden trenches and a disciplined volley of Martini-Henry fire crashed out. Warriors smashed to the ground. One Gcaleka survivor later described the moment as 'a sudden blaze' and recalled that 'our men fell like grass' (quoted in Gon 1979: 136). The British troops fired slowly and deliberately but still managed five aimed rounds a minute. The ground was soon littered with hundreds of fallen warriors. Amazingly, under such devastating fire, the Gcaleka held their ground, although further advance was impossible. Cover was sought behind every rock, bush and anthill. An early-morning mist descended and this, combined with the smoke emitted from the Martini-Henrys' black-powder cartridges, threw a brief veil over the battlefield. This allowed the Gcaleka to continue their attack and some were able to creep to within 100yd of the British trenches before the mist cleared. At this range the Martini-Henry fire was devastating; for 'F' and 'G' Companies of the 1/24th Regiment it was little more than rifle practice, with their former musketry instructor, Lieutenant Carrington, shouting encouragement. Soon even the brave Gcalekas could stand no more and the survivors broke and fled. It was a complete British victory.

Over 260 warriors were found dead near the British position, and it is thought a similwar number died in the bush of their wounds. The British lost not one man. Cunynghame was delighted by the performance of both the 1/24th Regiment and the Martini-Henry. He wrote of the troops' 'high state of drill and discipline and instruction' (quoted in Gon 1979: 140), which had made such a decisive victory possible. The Governor of the Cape, Sir Bartle Frere, wrote to the Colonial Secretary, Lord Carnarvon, to assert that the '24th are old, steady shots whose every bullet told' (quoted in Gon 1979: 140). Frere was also most complimentary about the performance of the Martini-Henry at Centane and, again in the same letter to Carnarvon, stressed the rifle's destructive power: 'They [the Gcaleka] came on in four divisions very steadily and in the days of the Brown Bess would certainly have closed, and being eight or ten to one would possibly have overwhelmed our people. They held on after several shells had burst among their advanced masses, but they could not live under the fire of the Martini-Henry' (quoted in David 2004: 34).

Royal Marine Light Infantry in marching order in 1875, with Martini-Henry Rifles Mark I, probably third-pattern. (Courtesy of Mrs B. Stadden)

Although the rebellious warriors would never again meet the British in a pitched battle, none of the rebellion's leaders, including Sandile, had been killed or captured at Centane and the conflict descended into a guerrilla war, during which the Swinburne-Henry Cavalry Carbine made a significant contribution. It was this weapon, rather than the Martini-Henry Cavalry Carbine Mark I, that saw service in the first months of the Anglo-Zulu War. Cunynghame, whose brisk manner had upset both his subordinates and the local politicians, was replaced by Major-General Sir Frederic Thesiger, soon to become, by inheritance, the 2nd Baron, Lord Chelmsford. Seeking refuge in the Amatola Mountains, between Grahamstown and King Williams Town, Sandile and the remaining rebels defied Thesiger's attempts to corner and defeat them for three long and arduous months. Eventually, by the continued reduction of the areas available to the rebels, the British were finally able to bring the 9th Cape Frontier War to a successful conclusion. It is clear that Thesiger found his first independent command difficult. He was frustrated that the Gcaleka refused to stand and fight, and by their ability to slip through the cordons that the British tried to establish. Thesiger viewed this action as pure cowardice on the part of the enemy, which allowed him to view the Gcalekas with undisguised racial contempt. Furthermore, Thesiger showed a deep reluctance to listen to the advice of the local white settlers, who had years of experience of this form of bush warfare, and these set views would later paralyze his initial planning for the Zulu campaign and would have fatal consequences for his command.

AFGHANISTAN

The 2nd Anglo-Afghan War (1878–81) saw the Martini-Henry in action in battles and skirmishes. The weapon was issued to regiments in India and destined for Afghanistan; for example, the Mark II was issued to the men of the 1/17th Regiment on 5 June 1877, just before they embarked for Afghanistan. The Martini-Henry would serve with distinction in this theatre, and on the North West Frontier, for more than 20 years in the hands of soldiers of the British Army and the Indian Army alike.

The first major engagement using the new Martini-Henry was undertaken by the Kurram Field Force, under the command of Major-General Frederick Roberts. On 1 December 1878, Roberts led a combined Indian and British Army force against a strong Afghan position at Peiwar Kotal. Although the 72nd Highlanders, armed with the Martini-Henry, were part of an assault force, it was their colleagues of the 5th Gurkhas, armed with the Snider-

OPPOSITE The attack on the Peiwar Kotal, Afghanistan, by the 5th Gurkha Rifles. The Gurkhas, advancing with Snider-Enfield rifles and fixed Pattern 1860 'Yataghan' Sword Bayonets up a wooded hillside, contrast with the British soldier of the 72nd Highlanders in the foreground, who carries a Martini-Henry rifle. (National Army Museum)

Enfield, who cleared the enemy from their entrenched positions. After the success of Peiwar Kotal and the capture of the fort of Ali Masjid, the British were able to impose some stability on the country and a British mission was installed in Kabul. However, a further Afghan uprising, and the brutal murder of all those in the British residency in September 1879, saw British and Indian troops return to the country in significant numbers, not only to restore order but to seek revenge for the killings.

Several major battles occurred over the next 15 months. At the battle of Charasia on 5 October 1879 Roberts found his route to Kabul barred by a numerically superior Afghan force. Roberts sent the 72nd Highlanders on a flanking march to attack the weak Afghan right, while the 92nd Highlanders supported this movement with an uphill assault of the main enemy defences. With Indian and Gurkha forces supporting both attacks, the Afghans gave way and were pursued from the battlefield by British and Indian cavalry units. Roberts entered a silent and sullen Kabul on 8 October.

Roberts wasted no time in dispensing summary justice against the ringleaders of the recent uprising. With winter approaching, the small garrison of 7,000 effectives established a defensive position in the partly fortified Sherpur cantonment, near to the city walls. Resentful of the British presence, thousands of Afghans from all over the country answered their mullah's call for a jihad against the infidel and hordes began to converge on Kabul. Hopelessly outnumbered, Roberts fortified Sherpur as best he could and awaited the onslaught.

This duly came on 23 December, when over 60,000 Afghans assaulted the cantonment. From the early hours to around midday, waves of attacks were launched by fanatical Afghans against the thinly spread British and Indian forces. At some points, the fighting was so intense that every rifle, Martini-Henry and Snider-Enfield, was in action; troops could simply not fire fast enough as the enemy hurled themselves at the position. British case-shot and high explosives burst over the attackers; Gatling guns rang out and the hot barrels of the Martini-Henrys glowed in the dark. This relentless fire kept the Afghans at bay and none was able to threaten the walls. By dawn, after hours of almost continuous firing, many of the Highland troops had shoulders so bruised by the recoil of their Martini-Henrys that they were forced to switch sides and continue firing from their other shoulder. Despite the pain and discomfort, and the danger of the situation, the Highlanders could joke that at least if they felt the pain it meant that they were still alive!

By mid-morning small groups of attackers began to melt away from the battlefield, and by noon Roberts was able to unleash his cavalry to dislodge the final stubborn fighters. It had been a crushing British victory. For the loss of just five killed, the defenders dispatched over 3,000 Afghans. It was a success built on the courage of both British and Indian defenders and the killing power of the Snider-Enfield and the Martini-Henry, which had taken a frightful toll on the attackers. At a range of roughly 400yd, where the Martini-Henry was at its most effective, a wall of Afghan bodies was found.

Although set-piece battles were a feature of the 2nd Anglo-Afghan War, so were small skirmishes; these frequently occurred when British units were on patrol. For example, on 24 March 1879, the 1/17th Regiment marched out of the town of Barihab, 11 miles south of Jellalabad, to destroy a number of villages nearby, from which local tribesmen had been harassing British troops. The villagers offered little resistance as the British burnt their homes, but, as the force returned to Barihab, thousands of tribesmen appeared from the surrounding hills and descended upon the valley floor to attack the British. This was the first occasion that the 1/17th Regiment fired their newly acquired Martini-Henry rifles, and the commanding officer, Lieutenant-Colonel William Dalrymple Thompson, recorded his thoughts on the effectiveness of the weapon:

Men of the 1/25th Regiment, Ali Musjid, Afghanistan, 1880, displaying their Martini-Henry rifles and an interesting collection of clothing to keep out the Afghan winter. (Courtesy of Ian Knight)

It is interesting to note that the fire of the men was slow, steady and effective. The average number of rounds of ammunition expended by the Battalion was 24 rounds per man. The enemy acknowledge a loss of 100 killed. There were none [casualties] in the Infantry. This extraordinary result may be attributed to:

1. The great defensive power of the Martini Henry Rifle in keeping the enemy at a distance [not one Afghan got within 400yd of the British firing line].
2. The wretched armament of the enemy. (LRO 22D63/32 1878–81: 115)

The Martini-Henry's firepower and range had clearly made a favourable impression upon the Colonel and presumably the troops of the 1/17th Regiment.

Other significant battles during this campaign included Ahmad Khel (19 April 1880) and Maiwand (27 July 1880). In the former, a surprise attack by 3,000 Afghans almost met with success as the British troops were unable to form square or fire sufficient volleys before the enemy were upon them. Even so, Private John Facer of the 30th Regiment was able to record, 'Our skirmishing line was at once thrown out, it is reinforced by supports and reserves, and you may guess a tremendous fire was kept up for a few minutes, and our Martini Henris [sic] did frightful execution. As they [the enemy] approached, the men instantly fixed bayonets for a death struggle' (NAM 8301/131). Facer also wrote of the hand-to-hand fighting and graphically described the reach of the Martini-Henry and bayonet: '... he was making a cut at me with a sword when he stumbled, and my bayonet entered his navel

37

and came out of his throat which put the fix on him' (NAM 8301/131). The courage and discipline exhibited by Facer and his comrades meant they were able to restore the firing line and beat back the Afghan assault.

At Maiwand, however, the British and Indian forces were not so fortunate. Having stumbled upon a large Afghan force armed with vastly superior artillery, the British commander, Burrows, failed to appreciate either the seriousness of the situation or the terrain over which he was fighting. Confusion and indecision reigned and although the Martini-Henry volleys of the 66th Regiment managed to keep the Afghans at bay for several hours, the Afghan artillery forced back the British guns and battered the British firing line. Eventually, the British position collapsed; the soldiers of the 66th Regiment were overwhelmed and, forming a last desperate square, were massacred to a man. Nearly 1,000 men from Burrows' command were left upon the battlefield and the Martini-Henrys of the 66th Regiment became great prizes for the victors. Despite this crushing defeat and loss of men, it should not be forgotten that the 2,476 troops of Burrows' command, with their Snider-Enfields and Martini-Henrys, inflicted over 5,000 casualties on the Afghan force.

THE ANGLO-ZULU WAR, 1879

According to historian John Laband, Thesiger's experiences in the Eastern Cape led him to over-confidence. At the start of the Zulu campaign, in January 1879, Thesiger, now Lord Chelmsford, and many of his command, presumed that the Zulus would be an adversary only slightly superior to those the British had fought in the Eastern Cape (Laband 1995: 208). The renowned British artist and war correspondent Melton Prior (1845–1910) recorded a meeting that Chelmsford held towards the end of the 9th Cape Frontier War with many of the Boers who had fought alongside the British. When the subject of a possible war with the Zulus was discussed, it is clear that Chelmsford was disdainful of the advice that the British must *laager*, or entrench, every position once they had crossed into Zulu territory, to avoid the danger of a surprise attack. The locals also stressed the mobility of the Zulu army and that in this regard the British should consider the Zulus as almost a cavalry force and deploy accordingly. Prior noted that Chelmsford responded to the Boers' pleading with the words, 'Oh, British troops are all right; we do not need to *laager* ...' and that the General 'smiled at the notion' (Prior 1912: 137).

The Boers had many years of experience fighting the mobile Zulu forces. Their success at the battle of Blood River on 16 December 1838 had become part of Boer folklore. From behind *laagered* wagons, fewer than 500 Boers held off repeated attacks from several thousand Zulus. Over 500 warriors were later found dead and hundreds more were killed in the subsequent flight and pursuit, for only three wounded Boer casualties. To the Boers, it was clear that sustained, accurate fire from behind a strong defensive position was the tactic to defeat the enveloping attack of the Zulu army.

Fostered by his experiences in the 9th Cape Frontier War, Chelmsford's initial concern was that it would be difficult to bring the Zulu army to battle.

Again, Chelmsford showed his reluctance to listen to local advice. John Dunn, a frontier settler who had lived in Zululand and had enjoyed some influence in the Zulu king Cetewayo's court, advised Chelmsford to divide his available force into two columns, each strong enough to defeat the Zulu army if engaged separately. According to Dunn, Lord Chelmsford laughed at this idea, and said, 'The only thing I am afraid of is that I won't get Cetywayo to fight' (quoted in Moodie 1886: 29).

Chelmsford thus resolved to use the 17,000 troops at his disposal to invade Zululand in three separate columns, with a fourth and fifth held back to bolster the defences of the boundary between Natal and Zululand and supply reinforcements if required. The three advancing columns would converge on the Zulu capital at Ulundi. Chelmsford hoped that at least one column would be able to meet the Zulu army in a pitched battle or that the Zulu king, Cetewayo, would defend his capital. Furthermore, Chelmsford placed a high emphasis on the proven killing power of the Martini-Henry. Writing to one of his more enlightened officers, Colonel Wood, on 23 November 1878, Chelmsford stated, 'I am inclined to think that the first experience of the power of the Martini-Henrys will be such a surprise to the Zulus that they will not be formidable after the first effort.'

Lance-corporal of the 3/60th Rifles, Anglo-Zulu War, 1879. He appears to carry a Martini-Henry Rifle Mark II with Pattern 1856 Sword Bayonet. Battalions such as the 3/60th Rifles would have been issued with the Mark II before other regiments. (Courtesy of The Royal Green Jackets (Rifles) Museum)

The success of the Martini-Henry at the battle of Centane had bred overconfidence in the British command, who believed that the Zulus would likewise be stopped by the rifle's punishing firepower. The British invaded Zululand on 11 January 1879 and, on the following day, the Central (No. 3) Column first engaged the enemy in a successful attack on Prince Sihayo's stronghold, which was subsequently burnt. The pace of the advance was now determined by the ponderous speed of the oxen-drawn wagon train that accompanied the British, and it was not until 20 January that the British column finally formed a camp at the base of a hill named iSandlwana. The rocky nature of the ground made the digging of defensive trenches impractical and the marshalling of the oxen to form a *laager* was considered but rejected as being too time consuming and difficult, given that this was to be a temporary camp. On the evening of 21 January, Chelmsford received reports of a concentration of Zulus in the Mangeni gorge, 12 miles east of the camp. He resolved to lead a reconnaissance force and, at 4am on 22 January, he left iSandlwana with six companies of the 2/24th Regiment, four Royal Artillery 7-pdr guns and a detachment of mounted infantry. The camp was left under the command of Lieutenant-Colonel H. Pulleine, who had at his disposal five companies of the 1/24th Regiment, one of the 2/24th Regiment, two 7-pdr guns and more than 100 mounted infantry. Before departing, Chelmsford ordered No. 2 Column, commanded by Lieutenant-Colonel A. Durnford, with units of the Natal Native Horse and the Natal Native Contingent, to move from Rorke's Drift to the iSandlwana camp. If attacked, Pulleine was instructed by Chelmsford to keep his cavalry vedettes (patrols) advanced, draw in his line of outposts and defend the camp. Including Durnford's force, Pulleine had a total of 67 officers and 1,707 men at his disposal.

The mobility and speed of advance for which the Zulu army was so renowned were demonstrated during the march to face British troops of No. 3 (Central) Column. Leaving Ulundi on 17 January, the main Zulu army had arrived, completely undetected, in the Ngwebeni Valley, just a few miles north of iSandlwana, on 21 January. While Chelmsford led half his force away from the Zulu army, the warriors rested and prepared for an attack on the camp at iSandlwana on 23 January. However, a cavalry patrol from the British position discovered the sheltering enemy by chance, and this triggered the events that followed. As the British galloped back to report the presence of a large Zulu army to the north of the camp, the Zulus quickly formed into regimental formations and boldly advanced on iSandlwana.

The Zulu army rapidly formed into its usual battle formation of 'chests and horns' as it moved on the British camp. While those regiments that formed the 'chest', supported by the tactical reserve that formed the 'loins', made a frontal attack, the warriors of the two 'horns' would swing round the hill of iSandlwana, unseen by the defending British, and envelop the position, surrounding them and cutting off any possible retreat. One of the few British survivors of the subsequent battle of iSandlwana, Lieutenant Henry Curling, Royal Artillery, later wrote of the complacency in the camp at the sight of the advancing Zulus:

> We congratulated ourselves on the chance of our being attacked and hoped that our small numbers might induce the Zulus to come on ... I suppose that not more than half the men in the camp took part in its defence as it was not considered necessary... The 1/24th had been in the last war and had often seen large bodies of Caffirs before. Not one of us dreamt that there was the least danger and all we hoped for was the fight might come off before the General [Chelmsford] returned... All the time we were idle in the camp, the Zulus were surrounding us with a huge circle several miles in circumference and hidden by hills from our sight. We none of us felt the least anxious as to the result for, although they came on in immense numbers, we felt it was impossible they could force a way through. (Curling 2001: 89–90)

Pulleine, in his first and last engagement, followed his orders to defend the camp to the letter and his initial dispositions reflected Chelmsford's wishes. The companies of the 24th Regiment fell in in columns in front of the British tents and the two 7-pdr guns were placed out to the left front of the camp. Durnford's arrival complicated the defence for, as senior officer, he seems to have decided to act independently and took his horsemen out roughly one mile to the right of the camp to engage the Zulus. It might have been that

Durnford felt there was a danger that the Zulus might simply bypass the camp and attack Chelmsford's column in the rear. Whatever Durnford's thinking, his troops were soon engaged with the Zulu advance. The defence of the camp was far from concentrated and much would depend on the killing power of the Martini-Henry rifle.

Initially, the British defences remained strong. The troops in the firing line remained steady as their Martini-Henry rifles checked the Zulu advance. Captain Edward Essex, one of only five imperial officers to survive, later wrote: 'I was surprised how relaxed the men in the ranks were despite the climactic tension of the battle. Loading as fast as they could and firing into the dense black masses that pressed in on them, the men were laughing and chatting, and obviously thought they were giving the Zulus an awful hammering' (quoted in Emery 1983: 80).

Despite Essex's assertion that the troops were 'loading as fast as they could' this would have gone against the training that the men would have received. The last *Musketry Instruction Manual* had been published in 1874 with the result that the troops fighting in 1879 had been trained according to principles that had been learnt from the use of the Snider-Enfield rifle (Knight 2002: 1). The 1874 manual emphasised slow, controlled and accurate fire and further evidence seems to suggest that this is how the men of the 24th fired at iSandlwana. With the smaller bore of the Martini-Henry allowing the men to carry around 70 cartridges (men armed with the Snider-Enfield had carried 40 to 50), the idea that the British firing line collapsed due to lack of ammunition seems implausible. Furthermore, the myth that began in Donald Morris's 1965 work, *The Washing of the Spears*, that British fire was reduced because ammunition boxes were difficult to open and thus re-supply was delayed, was disproved by archaeological research at iSandlwana in 2000.

Subsequent battles would suggest that the British fired in a slow and controlled way, just as they would have been trained. There seems little reason to conclude that the troops at iSandlwana, the 'old steady shots of the 1/24th', as Frere had earlier described them, would have been any different. Indeed, the musketry training of the day, for good reason, stressed slow, controlled fire. Rapid fire would have resulted in troops not taking careful aim, and the target would soon have been obscured by dense clouds of smoke from the black-powder cartridges. Slow fire allowed the men to select their targets carefully, and officers could more easily direct their fire as the targets moved or altered.

Volley fire, by section or company, could be carefully controlled and, in the heat of battle, the psychological effect of being at the receiving end could be just as discouraging as the casualties such fire inflicted. In such a battle as iSandlwana, and in subsequent engagements throughout the

Lieutenants R.W. Vause (left) and C. Raw (right) of the Natal Native Horse, Zululand, 1879. The photograph illustrates how the Martini-Henry Cavalry Carbine Mark I was held in its leather sling so that it could be mounted to the shoulder quickly. However, the weapon here is a Martini-Henry rifle, probably used due to a shortage of Martini-Henry carbines and the distrust of the jam-prone Swinburne-Henry carbine. Lieutenant Raw was the officer who first encountered the Zulu *impi* close to iSandlwana on 22 January 1879. (Courtesy of Adrian Greaves)

war, there would have been 'long pauses when some companies did not fire at all, either to allow the smoke to clear, or because they had no targets, the enemy having changed position or gone to ground' (Knight 2010: 378).

During the battle of Khambula in March 1879, British fire averaged only 33 rounds per man in four hours' action and at the final battle, Ulundi on 4 July 1879, only ten rounds were fired per man. An average of ten rounds was also expended at Gingindlovu on 2 April 1879. Similarly, average expenditure at Laing's Nek and Ingogo during the 1st Anglo-Boer War in January and February 1881 was 17 and 19 rounds respectively. At the furious battle of Tamai in the Sudan on 13 March 1884, where the Dervishes broke into the British square, the average expenditure per man was still only 50 rounds. Morris claims the 115 fit men defending Rorke's Drift fired about 20,000 rounds over ten hours, but this still equates to only 17.5 rounds per man per hour (Morris 1965: 416).

At the receiving end of this slow controlled fire from the Martini-Henry rifles, the attacking Zulus were suffering dreadful casualties. The British bullets tore through the hide shields of the Zulus and into the flesh of the warriors. Many were sent tumbling backwards by the impact of the bullets. Limbs were shattered or heads 'blown open like pumpkins' (Knight 2010: 374). Even 50 years after the battle, in the *Natal Mercury* of 22 January 1929, one Zulu veteran named Zimema could still recall the shock of his first exposure to the British fire: 'Some of our men had their arms torn right off... The battle was so fierce that we had to wipe the blood and the brains of the killed and wounded from our heads, faces, arms, legs and shields after the fighting ...'.

As the iNgobamakhosi regiment advanced to support the first Zulu attack, the warriors rushed forward in short bursts, throwing themselves down to try to avoid the volley fire. One Zulu, named Mehlokazulu, explained to the missionary Reverend A.W. Lee how he had advanced with 20 comrades only to be caught by volley fire. Only he was left standing (Knight 2010: 375). Mlamula Matebula, also of the

The battle of Khambula (previous pages)

This plate illustrates the moment at around 1.30pm when Colonel Redvers Buller and the men of the Frontier Light Horse (FLH) under his command returned to the safety of the British entrenched position at Khambula after they had successfully provoked the early attack of the Zulu 'right horn'. Buller is seen speaking to the British commander, Colonel Evelyn Wood, as men of the 90th Light Infantry aim their Martini-Henry rifles, the majority of which would have been Mark I, with some Mark II variants, at the rapidly approaching iNgobamakhosi regiment. Buller is shown holding a Swinburne-Henry Carbine; the Martini-Henry Cavalry Carbine was not issued to troops in South Africa until April 1879. The volley fire of the 90th halted the Zulu charge at a distance of 400yd from the British position, from where the Zulus directed uncoordinated fire upon the British. Although the Zulu force was to launch a series of courageous attacks against the British position for nearly four hours, by provoking the attack of the right horn the British were able to repel these uncoordinated attacks and claim a notable victory.

iNgobamakhosi regiment, described in the Zulu newspaper *Ilanga Lase Natal* on 20 June 1936 how the warriors tried to avoid the crippling fire:

> I with many others, adopted the style of crouching as we advanced in order to avoid the bullets as our shields could not stop them. While crouching I received a wound on my back, the bullet entered over the shoulder blade and came out lower down ... We fell down by hundreds, but we still advanced, although we were dying by hundreds we could not retreat because we had encircled them.

Lieutenant (later General Sir) Horace Smith-Dorrien, another of the five imperial officers who was to survive the battle, supplied the firing line with ammunition during the battle and commented on the 24th's performance: 'Possessed of a splendid discipline and sure of success, they lay on their position making every round tell' (Smith-Dorrien 1925: 83). Of course this was a wild exaggeration. In tense battlefield conditions, with smoke obscuring the targets and the Zulus doing everything in their power to avoid being hit, it took a surprisingly high number of rounds to kill or incapacitate a single enemy. Ian Knight has estimated a figure in the region of 40 or 50 rounds fired for every hit (Knight 2010: 385). Although the men of the 24th Regiment were above-average shots there is no reason to suggest that the figure would have been significantly lower. However, there is no doubt such sustained fire deterred any further Zulu advance, which became stalled 300–400yd from the British firing line, at a range when fire from the Martini-Henry was at its most effective and accurate. In an account preserved in the Symons Papers, Killie Campbell Collection, held at the University of KwaZulu-Natal, a Zulu veteran named uMhoti described how 'The soldiers ... in front of the camp poured volley after volley into the *impi* [formation] – we crouched down and dare not advance' (quoted in Knight 2010: 386). The Martini-Henry, the psychological effect of being under sustained volley fire, and the steadiness of the British troops, had checked the Zulu attack.

The sequence of events during the final stages of the battle of iSandlwana is hard to establish. Not only were there few British survivors, but many things happened either simultaneously or in quick succession. What seems clear is that Durnford's isolated command on the right flank of the British position was forced to retire to the camp as it was in danger of becoming outflanked and running low on ammunition, having left the camp with only around 40–50 rounds per man. This movement isolated Lieutenant Charles Pope's 'G' Company of the 2/24th Regiment, which had been sent forward by Pulleine to support Durnford. These infantrymen were quickly overwhelmed by the advancing Zulus and killed to a man. The remaining British firing line, seeing its right flank exposed, retreated towards the tent line, so as to concentrate its position and fire. The lull in the firing during this movement allowed the Zulus, just 300–400yd away, to seize their chance and charge at the British. The suddenness of the advance sparked fear in a detachment of the lightly armed Natal Native Contingent, who promptly discarded their weapons and fled for their lives. This resulted in a collapse of the firing line and, before the British

could re-form, the Zulus were upon them, stabbing and killing with their short assegai spears. Furthermore, the 'horns' swung around from behind the iSandlwana hill, cutting off any possible retreat for the British.

Only a very few mounted men managed to successfully flee the carnage. Of more than 1,700 men who had been in the British camp, only 60 white and about 400 black troops survived. Zulu losses are difficult to evaluate for there was never an accurate count, but it is clear that they were numerous. The Martini-Henry rifle had claimed at least 2,000 warriors, and scores, with terrible wounds, must have dragged themselves from the battlefield to die miles away. When the news of the Zulu victory and his nation's losses reached Cetewayo, he was heard to say: 'An assegai has been thrust into the belly of the nation... There are not enough tears to mourn for the dead' (Morris 1965: 387).

Elsewhere on 22 January 1879, the Martini-Henry rifle was claiming further Zulu victims. The British invasion force to the south, No. 1 Column, was under the command of Colonel Charles Pearson, who had been given the objective of crossing the Lower Drift of the Thukela River. His force, consisting of two British infantry battalions, the 2/3rd Regiment and the 99th Regiment, plus nearly 300 sailors of the Naval Brigade, complete with rocket tubes and a Gatling gun, was then to march the 30 miles to the mission station at Eshowe, where he was to establish a base from which he could coordinate a further advance towards Ulundi. By the morning of 22 January, Pearson was still some miles short of Eshowe, with his force split crossing over the Nyezane River. Waiting to ambush the British column were 6,000 Zulus, under the command of an inDuna (leader) named Umatyiya, concealed around the base of the Majia Hill. Fortunately for Pearson and his men, a reconnaissance patrol of the Natal Native Contingent stumbled across the hidden Zulus and the trap was sprung prematurely. The British reacted quickly and decisively – a firing line was rapidly formed, the artillery and rocket tubes brought into action and, for the first time in British military history, the Gatling gun fired in anger, in a short burst which had the desired effect of dispersing a formation of Zulus. Unlike at iSandlwana, the Zulu regiments failed to coordinate successfully, and, in particular, the attack of the 'horns' was not pressed home.

Again, the Martini-Henry rifle proved its worth, stopping the advance of the Zulu 'chest' in its tracks, as was later testified by Zulu survivors of the battle: 'The whites shot us down in numbers, in some places our dead and wounded covered the ground, we lost heavily, especially from the small guns [Martini-Henrys]' (quoted in Laband 1985: 85). The Zulus, largely armed as they were with antiquated firearms, many of them flintlocks, were unable to respond to the devastating British fire. 'We went forward packed close together like a lot of bees. We were still far away from them when the white men began to throw their bullets at us, but we could not shoot at them because our rifles would not shoot so far' (quoted in Greaves 2005: 231). The British, too, recognized the superiority of the Martini-Henry. Captain Fitzroy Hart, the commanding officer of the 2nd Regiment of the Natal Native Contingent, wrote that: 'The Zulus fought well, showing judgement and courage quite equal to their enemy, but although they outnumbered us greatly, they could not hold their ground against our artillery and superior rifles. We had the best rifles in the world; they, for the most part, merely muskets, weapons of the past' (quoted in Knight 2003: 60).

The British victory of arms and discipline was complete. For the loss of just 14 killed and 15 wounded, the British forces at Nyezane had inflicted well over 500 Zulu casualties. The British were to call upon the Martini-Henry again later in the day, when a Zulu army, 4,000 strong, fresh from its victory at iSandlwana, descended upon the British supply station at Rorke's Drift, defended by just 100 men of the 2/24th Infantry. From behind defences, the British were able not only to hold back numerous attacks, but to claim some 400 Zulu lives using the firepower of the Martini-Henry. The British were again fortunate that the Zulus possessed inferior weapons; if the Zulu fire from the Shiyane terraces, 330–440yd distant from the defences of Rorke's Drift, had been from Martini-Henry rifles, or even Snider-Enfields, then the British position would soon have become untenable. As it was, the defenders faced largely ineffectual fire from elderly muskets, many of which did not even have the range to reach the British barricades. Several soldiers, including Corporals Hitch and Allen of the 2/24th Regiment, were hit by Zulu bullets, yet survived wounds that would certainly have proved fatal if they had been inflicted by more modern rifles. In contrast, the British fire upon the terraces claimed several Zulu victims, as testified by Corporal Allen in the *Cambrian* newspaper on 13 June 1879: 'We fired many shots, and I said to my comrade, "They are falling fast over there", and he said "Yes, we are giving it to them." I saw many Zulus killed on the hill [Shiyane terrace].'

An old Zulu, photographed in the 1930s, holding a Martini-Henry rifle which he claimed to have taken from the battlefield of iSandlwana. The staff of the weapons department of the National Army Museum believe the rifle is the correct pattern, but it seems to have been modified at the forend. (Courtesy of Ian Knight)

A famous photograph of Boer leader Piet Uys Jr (1827–79) with his sons. Piet Uys Jr is holding a Swinburne-Henry Carbine, while his sons are holding Martini-Henry rifles, probably Mark Is, supplied to them by the British when they volunteered to join Colonel Evelyn Wood's No. 4 Column. Piet Uys was killed trying in vain to save one of his sons at the battle of Hlobane on 28 March 1879. (Courtesy Ian Knight)

However, the engagement at Rorke's Drift also demonstrated some of the inherent problems associated with the Martini-Henry. Private Alfred Henry Hook, one of the defenders of the hospital who was to receive a Victoria Cross for his heroism, commented that '… we did so much firing that [the rifles] became hot, and the brass of the cartridges softened, the result being that the barrels got very foul and the cartridge-chamber jammed. My own rifle was jammed several times' (quoted in Emery 1983: 130). Similarly, after prolonged use the rifle barrels became so hot that soldiers were forced to hold them away from their faces while firing, thus reducing their accuracy. Indeed, after the several hours of virtually constant fire endured by the defenders, it is hard to imagine how anyone could fire the rifle efficiently. Despite these drawbacks, the Martini-Henry rifle allowed the British to decisively defeat their foes and inflict horrific wounds upon them. Lieutenant John Merriott Chard, Royal Engineers, was impressed by the extraordinary wounds inflicted on the Zulus: 'One man's head was split open, exactly as if done with an axe. Another had been hit just between the eyes, the bullet carrying away the whole of the back of the head, leaving his face perfect, as though it were a mask, only disfigured by the small hole made by the bullet passing through' (quoted in Knight 1993: 108).

The British Government agreed to Chelmsford's urgent request for reinforcements and dispatched six battalions, two cavalry regiments and two artillery batteries to South Africa. On their arrival in March, Chelmsford felt strong enough to renew his offensive and, in particular, relieve Colonel Pearson and his men, who were besieged at the mission station of Eshowe. What tactical approach was Chelmsford going to take now? The lessons of iSandlwana, Nyezane and Rorke's Drift were numerous; the Zulu army was mobile and more determined, with great tactical awareness, than the British had first considered. If allowed to develop, the flanking movements of the Zulu 'horns' could be deadly to a static British firing line. Yet, the stopping power of the Martini-Henry had been evident throughout the campaign and Rorke's Drift had clearly demonstrated that from behind prepared defensive positions the British could defeat the numerically superior Zulu army. Further events served to clarify Chelmsford's thinking. In the early morning of 12 March 1879, a British force, which had failed to entrench their overnight camp at Intombi Drift, was surprised and overwhelmed by a Zulu attack, losing over 80 men. However, a fighting retreat by the British survivors successfully held the Zulus at bay with accurate and controlled fire from their Martini-Henrys.

Certainly, Chelmsford showed that he was capable of altering his tactics against the mobile flanking attacks of the Zulus. He decided upon the use of the 'square formation' long associated with the Napoleonic wars, where the use of infantry squares to deter and repel enemy cavalry attacks had been commonly used. The square would allow the British to concentrate the firepower of the Martini-Henry, provide cohesion and mutual support to the British infantrymen and also, crucially, nullify the Zulus' attempts to outflank the British firing line.

Chelmsford was not the only British commander to have learnt from the early engagements. The No. 4 Column, under Colonel Henry Evelyn Wood, operated as the northern advance column. Following the news of iSandlwana, Wood had taken a position upon raised ground at Khambula. Wood did not dismiss the Boer advice and the entrenched British position was well constructed, with the use of wagons as barricade defences. When a Zulu army, 20,000 strong, attacked on 29 March 1879, these defences were tested, but were not found wanting. This is especially significant as a number of the Zulus fired captured Martini-Henrys at the British, who were able to withstand the fire from behind the safety provided by the wagons. In return, the British were able to inflict over 2,000 casualties upon the charging Zulus with Martini-Henry and artillery fire. The British were able to provoke a premature attack by the right 'horn', thus hampering any Zulu attempts to coordinate their advance. Khambula was, undoubtedly, a crushing victory for the British which shattered Zulu morale. For historian John Laband, the battle of Khambula had many parallels with the battle of Blood River: 'though some forty years separated the two battles, they followed precisely the same pattern, the only difference being the improved firepower of the whites' (Laband 1995: 102).

Three days after Wood's victory, Chelmsford was also to enjoy success over the Zulus at the battle of Gingindlovu on 2 April. Determined to avoid the previous mistakes, Chelmsford led his Eshowe relief force of 5,670 men into Zululand on 29 March. The men travelled lightly, with no tents or baggage, and the march was careful and considered. Overnight camps were painstakingly laagered, with wagons packed into a tight square, and entrenched. Local advice and intelligence, particularly from John Dunn, was listened to and heeded. By midday on 1 April, Chelmsford and his men neared the vicinity of Nyezane. Scouts had reported the growing presence of larger groups of Zulus, and Pearson had, using a heliograph, been able to inform Chelmsford that a large Zulu army, in the region of 12,000 warriors, was being assembled to block the British advance on Eshowe. With the terrain and vegetation offering wonderful cover to the Zulus for a surprise attack, Chelmsford took no chances. John Dunn selected a position on the summit of a slight knoll to construct the British camp and later swam across the Nyezane River, under cover of darkness, to report to Chelmsford the presence of a large Zulu force. Dunn informed Chelmsford that in all probability the British would be attacked at dawn.

Writing in 1896, Colonel Callwell described the battle of Gingindlovu as a 'tactical defensive' engagement in which the Zulus, as at Khambula, assumed the offensive (Callwell 1896: 76). Indeed, the British position was certainly a strong defensive one. The wagon laager was formed over 140 sq yd, giving sufficient room inside to accommodate 2,000 oxen,

A Martini-Henry Rifle Mark II, once the rifle of Private Walters of the 1/24th Regiment. It was taken by the victorious Zulus at the battle of iSandlwana and used against the British at Khambula, where it was recovered. (Courtesy of Adrian Greaves)

300 horses and over 2,000 native troops. The 3,400 imperial troops were positioned in the enclosing shelter-trench, which was 172yd square and roughly 14yd from the laagered wagons. The corners, the weakest point, were reinforced by the placing of the 9-pdr guns, the Gatling guns and the rocket tubes. Although the British had worked tirelessly throughout the afternoon to prepare their strong defences, darkness and heavy rain, which was to soak the British throughout the night, meant it was not possible to cut back the high grasses and bush that encroached to within 100yd of the defences.

The Zulu force, commanded by Somopho, viewed the British position on the open plain as one that was ripe to be enveloped by the traditional tactics of the 'horns of the buffalo'. The Zulus crossed the Nyezane in columns at two drifts, separated by a distance of a mile or so. As they advanced up the slope towards the British position, the Zulus deployed into the 'chest and horns' formation; one column veered off to the left to form the left 'horn', the other fanned out to create the 'chest'. Suddenly, from around a knoll on the British left, known as Misi Hill, appeared the right 'horn'.

At a distance of 800yd a petty officer of HMS *Boadicea*, in charge of one of the Gatling guns, begged Lord Chelmsford's permission to test the range of the weapon. Chelmsford nodded his assent for a short burst, and at the turn of two handles, the Gatling's fire was directed at the charging Zulus. Although a clear lane was cut through the body of warriors, the fire did not slow the Zulu advance in the slightest. Within a few seconds the attackers had reached the 400yd distance markers that had been diligently placed out the night before. It would soon be the turn of the Martini-Henry to demonstrate its stopping power.

With cries of 'They are encircled!' and 'uSuthu!' the Zulu tried to close in on the British position. The first Zulu assault was upon the north side of the position, manned by soldiers of the 3/60th Rifles. Regaled with gruesome stories of the slaughter of iSandlwana, the young and inexperienced riflemen were now confronted by hordes of fearless warriors. Captain Edward Hutton of the 3/60th Rifles was not surprised that the first volley seemed so ineffectual, for it 'could hardly be expected to have done much execution, since there were but a number of darting figures at irregular intervals and distances' (quoted in Emery 1983: 201). Many troops simply froze or fired wildly. Officers, including Hutton, reacted quickly; some troops received a swift blow across the back from a parade-ground stick, others the venom of their officer's tongue. As Hutton wrote, 'a smart rap with my stick soon helped a man recover his self-possession' (quoted in Emery 1983: 201). Steadiness was restored and each man pushed another round into the breech of his Martini-Henry.

The British, according to Lieutenant E.O.H. Wilkinson of the 3/60th Rifles, were, at this early stage of the battle, 'volley-firing their rifles by sections' (quoted in Emery 1983: 196), which would have facilitated greater control of the firing line, maintained a more constant fire and allowed battlefield smoke to clear between volleys. Ian Knight has estimated that at long ranges of 700–1,400yd, volley fire was no more than 2 per cent effective in killing or wounding a charging adversary. At a medium range of 300–700yd, Knight claims that the effective percentage only rose to 5 per cent and at close range of 100–300yd, volley fire was 15 per cent effective. Knight believes that even this figure might be optimistic, for a huge amount of smoke would have obscured targets and adrenaline would have reduced accuracy further (Knight 2002: 4).

Martini-Henry bayonets

	Overall length	Blade length
Pattern 1853 Socket Bayonet	20.40in	16.90in
Pattern 1856 Sword Bayonet	28.18in	22.75in
Pattern 1858 Sword Bayonet	28.18in	22.75in
Pattern 1859 Cutlass Bayonet	32.50in	26.80in
Pattern 1860 Sword Bayonet	28.18in	22.75in
Pattern 1871 Cutlass Bayonet	31.30in	25.60in
Pattern 1876 Socket Bayonet	25.00in	21.75in
Pattern 1879 Sawback Bayonet	29.80in	24.30in
Pattern 1887 Sword Bayonet	23.75in	18.50in
Pattern 1895 Socket Bayonet	22.00in	17.50in

The reason for such low percentages can be explained by battlefield adrenaline combined with inexperience. Undoubtedly at Gingindlovu the inexperience of the troops, particularly the 3/60th Rifles, would have reduced the percentage of hits. John Dunn noted that the young soldiers were failing to adjust their rifle sights as the Zulus closed in on the British, with the result that many bullets would have sailed over the enemy's heads. Yet for all the failings of British marksmanship, the young British soldiers, and the Martini-Henry, achieved a crushing victory. Herein lies an important truth about the effectiveness of battlefield, particularly volley, fire. Again, as Knight has claimed:

> Killing the enemy was not the sole objective. Discouraging his attacks, breaking up his formations, and causing him to retire were the tactical necessities, and it was necessary to kill only a small proportion of the enemy involved to achieve them. To withstand prolonged and accurate Martini-Henry fire was a terrifying experience that even the bravest warrior could not endure indefinitely. (Knight 2002: 4)

Lieutenant Hutton noted that the 3/60th Rifles in their defence of the laager, fired fewer than seven rounds a man. Thus, approximately 4,000 rounds were fired by the 540 men of the 3/60th Rifles. After the battle 61 dead Zulus were found in the most destructive fire zone, opposite the 3/60th Rifles' position. It follows that over 60 rounds were fired for every Zulu killed, although this does not take into account the numbers wounded. Effectively the Zulu attack stalled, not because of high numbers of casualties in the attack, but because British volley fire created an impression of impenetrability. This view is supported by John Guy, who states, 'we cannot deny the physical damage and the demoralisation caused by British fire-power in Zululand' (Guy 1971: 570).

Colonel Callwell supports Hutton's claim for the number of rounds fired at Gingindlovu: 'Statistics show that a few rounds a man represents the amount in each fight … the expenditure was not over 10 rounds per man' (Callwell 1896: 396). Corporal John Hargreaves of the 3/60th Rifles recalled that 'Lord Chelmsford was on foot going round the Laager with a red night cap on, and encouraging the men, directing their fire and advising them to fire low and steady' (Lib. RGJ D.37). Such instructions were simply following the policy outlined by official training manuals, where slow fire was considered to be effective fire. Such steady, controlled volley fire again explains the low number of shots fired per man. Not all the British troops were indifferent shots. Lieutenant Wilkinson observed one marksman of the 3/60th Rifles drop 'four running Zulus at 400 yards with consecutive shots', while Hutton saw a group of ten to 15 Zulus run for the cover of a clump of palm bushes only for all them to be killed by a directed volley (Knight & Castle 1994: 198).

Taking cover in the long wet grass, the Zulus returned an ineffectual fire on the British square. Some of the warriors were armed with Martini-Henrys, plundered from the battlefield of iSandlwana, but fortunately for the British, the Zulu fire was mostly high. Apparently, the Zulus also had difficulty in adjusting the range sights. Although the Zulu fire claimed some notable victims, including Lieutenant George Johnson of the 99th Regiment and Colonel F.V. Northey of the 3/60th Rifles, the final British butcher's bill of 13 killed and 48 wounded was, considering the intensity of the battle, remarkably light. Chelmsford's decision to prepare shelter trenches undoubtedly saved the lives of many riflemen.

As the Zulu advance ground to a halt, the warriors comprising the 'chest' began to edge to their right, past the corner of the square, and attempted to attack the men of the 99th Regiment on the left face. The warriors of the left 'horn' had pushed forward to a point where they were able to make a determined attack upon the front right corner. It was here that one of the Gatling guns was placed and the 1,200 rounds it fired proved sufficient to beat back the attackers, although it was claimed one Zulu warrior managed to get close enough to the Gatling to actually touch it before being cut down. The Zulus moved further against the 99th Regiment. Their threat seemed so intense that even the special correspondent of the *Evening Standard*, Norris Newman, grabbed a Martini-Henry and claimed at least one Zulu victim. Again, as with the charge on the front face, the attack on the left stalled. At this point the right 'horn' appeared from Misi Hill and deployed to attack the rear face of the laager, defended by the men of the 91st Highlanders.

As inexperienced as their colleagues in the 3/60th Rifles, the men of the 91st Highlanders acquitted themselves well in their first engagement in Zululand. Their sights were adjusted down from 500 to 400, then 300, 200 and 100yd, and no Zulu got within 30yd of the shelter trenches. The Martini-Henry fire of the 91st Highlanders was ably supported by fire from two 9-pdrs and, at the other end of the line, a Gatling and rocket tubes. The British 'were able to put down a terrible barrier of fire around the square' (Knight & Castle 1994: 203), which made the Zulu attack recoil from the rear face and roll round to attack the right face, desperate to find any place to break into the defences and engage the British in hand-to-hand combat. Here, defence was left to the seasoned veterans of the 57th Regiment, who met the Zulu charge with steady, well-directed volley fire. The battle had now been raging for an hour and, although stalled, the Zulus showed no sign of retreating, but clung on to the cover afforded by the long grass and continued their sniping at the British. Chelmsford considered it was time to unleash Captain Barrow's Mounted Infantry, who filed out of the square and launched themselves upon the warriors of the right 'horn'. A few warriors made a determined stand and sold their lives, but the majority of their comrades fell back rapidly. Barrow later estimated that 50–60 Zulus fell in this mounted advance. Chelmsford then followed up this attack with the Natal Native Contingent, who were instructed to clear the field, a task they completed with relish. Many a wounded Zulu was dispatched by the marauding Natal Native Contingent, whose officers lost control of their men. As the surviving Zulus fled the battlefield, Chelmsford was able to claim a notable victory. Over 500 Zulu bodies were found close to the British square and a further 200 were discovered the following day. Total Zulu casualties were probably in excess of 1,200. The next day Chelmsford's column relieved Eshowe.

Lieutenant Hutton considered that the victory owed much to the Martini-Henry rifles, which he described as 'the most perfect weapons in the world' (quoted in Emery 1983: 201). In the *Sheffield Daily Telegraph* of 22 April 1879 a colour-sergeant of the 91st Regiment claimed that

Men of the 2/3rd Regiment guard Zulu prisoners after the battle of Gingindlovu, 2 April 1879. This image illustrates well the length of the Martini-Henry rifle, especially when the Pattern 1876 Socket Bayonet was attached. (Courtesy Ian Knight)

Bayonets

The most common bayonet used with the Martini-Henry rifle was the Pattern 1853 Socket Bayonet or 'common' bayonet as it was usually known, for practically every man in the rank and file used it. Originally this bayonet was introduced for use with the Pattern 1853 Enfield Rifle-Musket, which was a muzzle-loader, so the triangular blade of this bayonet was slightly curved away from the barrel when mounted. This allowed the soldier to reload without the danger of injuring himself on the point of the blade, which could happen if the blade was straight. It was also used with the Snider-Enfield arm. The Pattern 1853 bayonet was carried in a leather scabbard with brass fittings. To fit it to the smaller-diameter Martini-Henry barrel, it was necessary to braze a bushing (a metal cylinder) into the socket.

As stocks of the Pattern 1853 bayonet began to run down, the Government took the opportunity to introduce the Pattern 1876 Socket Bayonet. Longer, at 25in, with a blade that was now equiangular in cross-section rather than having a wider top flat, this bayonet became affectionately known as 'the lunger' by British troops for, when combined with the rifle, it gave them a reach of over 6ft and thus a distinct advantage in close combat.

The Pattern 1860 Sword Bayonet was one of a series of sword bayonets used with the Martini-Henry, commencing with the Pattern 1856, which had been used with the Snider-Enfield Short Rifle (with a 30.5in barrel, as opposed to the 36.5in barrel of the Long Rifle) issued to Rifle regiments and sergeants of the line-infantry regiments, and with some artillery carbines. Again the socket had to be bushed to accommodate the smaller diameter of the Martini-Henry's muzzle. The sword bayonets were all of a common form, with a recurving blade known as a 'Yataghan' type, so that name has often been applied to them as a generic term.

The Pattern 1859 Cutlass Bayonet, used by Royal Marines, was based on the design of a ship's cutlass, with a basket hilt and a heavy, slightly curved blade. Once more, it had to be modified for use with the Martini-Henry rifle; the Pattern 1871 Cutlass Bayonet was a simple conversion of the Pattern 1859 bayonet, with a shorter and straighter blade (the Pattern 1859 was 32.5in in total with a blade 26.8in long, while the Pattern 1871 was 31.3in long with a blade measuring 25.6in). A specific bayonet was also produced for the Martini-Henry Artillery Carbine Mark I, which was a variation of the Pattern 1859 Cutlass Bayonet. The most significant feature was the addition of a 9.25in saw on the upper side of the blade.

'Nothing in the world could stand our fire', while on 28 April 1879 the *Perthshire Advertiser* printed a soldier's letter which claimed that ' At Ginghilovo our Martini-Henrys swept away the Zulus like a broom'. It seems clear that these first-hand accounts influenced the thinking of the editors of British newspapers, many of whom clearly felt that Chelmsford's victory was as a result of a superiority of firepower over the Zulus and the inability of the enemy to alter their tactics. For example, on 26 April 1879 the *Essex Standard* stated:

> Our forces stood depending on their breechloaders entirely, to repel the assault. The Zulus on their part, true to their usual tactics, attempted another surprise, and early in the morning, in force it would appear about 11,000 strong, attempted to carry the British camp by storm, rushing down upon it in two separate bodies from the surrounding heights. The struggle lasted but for an hour or so, but was very desperate, the enemy, with a daring valour that it is impossible not to admire, sweeping onward in their assault amid the pitiless hail of rifle bullets which they had to face... Thus it will be seen, that it was the steady and well-directed fire of our Riflemen that repulsed the attack, and the experience of the battle shows that against this the soldiers of Cetewayo cannot stand.

Similarly, on 26 April 1879 the editor of the *Isle of Man News* wrote: 'We may suppose, then, that it will be claimed that we have scored a

Pattern 1876 'Lunger' Socket Bayonet 0.22in. The blade was now equiangular in cross section, rather than having a wider top flat. The leather scabbard has brass mounts. (Courtesy of Jonathan R. Hope)

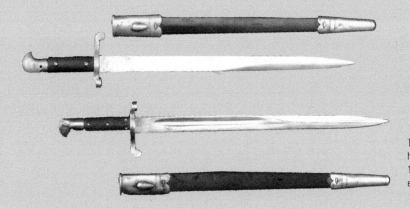

The left-hand-side (top) and the right-hand-side (bottom) of the Pattern 1887 Martini-Henry Sword Bayonet, each with leather scabbard. (Author)

victory in Zululand, although, technically, it is simply a successful defence from a sudden and determined attack, due principally to our possession and skilful use of Martini-Henry rifles, Gatling guns, rocket tubes, and other ghastly apparatus of death.'

The fire of the Martini-Henry presented a huge psychological barrier to the Zulu advance. The horrendous wounds the bullets could inflict and the certainty that any advance would be met by crushing volley fire meant that the Zulu attack stalled at a range of 300yd from the British square. Perhaps this was the ultimate test of the rifle's stopping-power, if not 'killing power'. The biggest factor in the British success was Chelmsford's decision to alter his tactics and entrench his force in a defensive square, so as to nullify the flanking attacks of the Zulus, and maximize the concentration of fire from the Martini-Henrys. The enemy obliged Chelmsford by not altering their tactics, which allowed him to direct the destructive British firepower in a concentrated manner.

Chelmsford's victory, and the tactics deployed, were repeated in the final battle of the Anglo-Zulu War, at Ulundi on 4 July 1879. The combined forces of the 2nd Division and Wood's Flying Column assembled in an infantry square, or more accurately a parallelogram formation, upon the Mahlabathini plain and marched slowly on their target of Ulundi. Chelmsford was insistent that the Zulus be finally defeated in the open, rather than from behind a defensive laager, so as to demonstrate to the Zulus that any further resistance would be futile and show the superiority of the British soldier. Such a disposition risked higher casualties from Zulu

Troops of the 2/21st Regiment at the site where the Prince Imperial, Emperor Napoleon III's only son, was killed – Sobhuza's homestead. The photograph, taken on either 2 or 3 June 1879, shows the men of the 2/21st Regiment with their Martini-Henry rifles. (Courtesy of Ian Knight)

rifle fire, but earlier battles had shown Zulu marksmanship to be poor and there was no reason to believe that it would pose any real threat.

As the British edged forward, the Zulu army of 15,000–20,000 warriors was first seen approaching at around 8.30am. A screen of British cavalry on each flank ensured that the usual enemy tactical formation of the 'chest and the horns' could not be successfully deployed. Furthermore, accurate artillery fire smashed into any large congregations of Zulus, again making a concerted attack difficult. The face of the advancing square was manned by the men of the 80th Regiment, supported by Gatlings, 7-pdrs and 9-pdrs. Despite the disruptive artillery fire, the Zulus were able to approach to within range of the Martini-Henry rifles. The British infantry, with two front ranks kneeling and two ranks standing behind, opened a fearful volley fire by sections. Corporal William Roe of the 58th Regiment wrote, 'They [the Zulus] were falling down in heaps, as though they had been tipped off carts' (quoted in David 2004: 348). The British fire ensured, as one corporal of the 90th Light Infantry quoted in the *Manchester Guardian* of 6 September 1879 claimed, that the Zulus went to ground and remained at 'a respectful distance'. The Zulus now unleashed sniper fire upon the British square which the war artist Melton Prior described as 'very warm' and it was now that the majority of the British casualties occurred (Laband & Knight 1996: 139). Grenadier Guards officer 2nd Lieutenant R. Wolrige Gordon wrote of the Zulu fire as well as the power of the Martini-Henry:

> The battle began, and in a short time there was such a rain of bullets flying over our heads that it was, as one of the men remarked, 'for all the world like a hailstorm'. I remained standing, watching the battle through my field glasses. It was a curious sight, and one could plainly see men, when hit, throw up their arms and fall. The thud a bullet makes against a man's body is a most curious sound. (ASHM N-C91. GOR.W)

As at Gingindlovu, the wall of fire surrounding the British square largely stalled the Zulu attack. Only at the rear corner of the square, where the

58th and 2/21st Regiments were deployed, did a rush of Zulu warriors really threaten the British and here the attack got to within 30yd. Chelmsford was there at the critical moment and Melton Prior heard the general say to his troops, 'Men, fire faster, can't you fire faster?' Prior was rather disdainful of Chelmsford when he wrote in his autobiography, 'Now it is not my business to question the wisdom of this remark, but I cannot help contrasting it with Lord Wolseley's well-known order. "Fire, slow, fire slow!"' (Prior 1912: 145). Once the threat had been repulsed, Chelmsford repeated his tactic of Gingindlovu and unleashed troopers from the 17th Lancers and Mounted Infantry to rout the enemy. The battle had lasted a mere half-hour. British casualties were ten dead and 69 wounded. There is no accurate figure for the Zulu dead, but over 1,000 bodies were found around the British square and along the path of the cavalry pursuit. Ulundi was burned to the ground and Chelmsford had effectively brought the war to an end.

Once again, the expenditure of Martini-Henry ammunition was low, at an average of 6.4 rounds per man, despite Chelmsford's pleas for his men to fire faster at a critical moment. For all the bravery of the Zulu nation, the British Army had decisively defeated their enemy, both from behind prepared defences and out on an open plain. Despite the over-confidence in the tactical superiority of the Martini-Henry at the start of the conflict, Chelmsford had had the foresight to alter his tactical deployments so as to neutralize the tactics of the Zulu army and best use the power of the Martini-Henry rifle. Indeed the Martini-Henry's famed stopping power was proven during the war, even if it did not claim as many victims as the soldiers who fired it, and the historians who first wrote of the conflict, had initially thought. The psychological effect of Martini-Henry volley fire is difficult to measure but it is clear that such fire repeatedly stalled attacks. It is worth noting that the majority of Martini-Henry rifles that saw service in the Anglo-Zulu War would have been third-pattern Mark Is, as the process of adapting these weapons to the Mark II pattern had really only just begun. The robustness, simplicity and stopping power of the Martini-Henry was appreciated by the troops

British outpost at Pretoria, 1881, during the 1st Anglo-Boer War. Note the picquets in the background with Martini-Henry Rifles Mark II. (Courtesy of Ian Knight)

who used the weapon in anger in 1879, and this admiration would be carried over into the battles of the 1880s.

Although the Martini-Henry saw service during the 1st Anglo-Boer War (1880–81), the dispersed nature of the enemy, who were experts in using cover, and the defensive terrain that the conflict was fought over, meant that the weapon was unable to effectively demonstrate its qualities. Pitted against Boer rifles, such as the .441in Westley Richards, the Martini-Henry's range was not sufficient to dominate the battlefield. Nor were the British able to concentrate their firepower in volley fire. A combination of poor generalship, ineffective intelligence and weak political leadership saw this short war brought to a humiliating conclusion.

EGYPT AND THE SUDAN

By 1881, with many of the initial problems with the Mark I resolved, H.P. Miller, assistant musketry instructor to the National Rifle Association, was able to conclude that the 'regulation Martini-Henry Rifle is a sound, reliable, and accurate military arm. This is certainly my experience' (Miller 2010: 23). The Martini-Henry Mark II was far superior to any firearm previously issued to the British Army. The fact that the Martini-Henry had a smaller bore than the Snider-Enfield meant soldiers could carry more ammunition (Scarlata 2004: 36). Greater accuracy, lower trajectory, ease of operation and reloading with consequent rapidity of firing, as well as its robustness, all combined to make the Martini-Henry a solid, if not always completely dependable, weapon.

It was felt that the weapon certainly possessed the necessary 'stopping power' that the British Army required against the 'savage foes' of colonial warfare. The seven-grooved barrel, and the 85 grains of black powder in the .450in Boxer-type cartridge, allowed the hardened-lead bullet of 480 grains to emerge with a muzzle velocity of 1,350ft/sec, rising in a curved trajectory of 8.1ft at a range of 500yd. This compared to a trajectory of 11.9ft for the Snider and 15ft for the Enfield over the same range. Thus the accuracy of the Martini-Henry was much improved over the two former rifle stalwarts of the British Army (Featherstone 1978: 24). The Martini-Henry was sighted to 1,000yd and, in the hands of a trained marksman, could maintain a reasonable degree of accuracy at that range. Battalion volley fire against massed targets frequently opened at 600–800yd, and even an average rifleman could score a high percentage of hits at 300–400yd, where volley fire could be particularly devastating (Morris 1965: 297). A bullet fired from the rifle at 40yd could penetrate a sandbag to a depth of nearly 12in. In practice, the hardened-lead bullet could stop a charging warrior in his tracks; the slug smashed anything in its path, and inflicted small entry holes with horrific exit wounds. In experienced hands ten to 12 'aimed' volleys could be fired per minute into the charging ranks of a massed enemy (Knight 1991: 22).

In 1882 a British expeditionary force under the command of General Sir Garnet Wolseley was dispatched to Egypt to quell a nationalist uprising and secure the British hold on the Suez Canal. In this conflict the Martini-Henry would be up against the modern .433in Remington rifle as used by the Egyptian Army. Although an effective weapon, the Remington lacked the range of the Martini-Henry (the Remington had a maximum range of 800yd and an effective range of 200–300yd) and at short distances the Egyptian troops had a tendency to aim high, as even those who did possess sights did not adjust them properly. At the battle of Kassassin (28 August 1882), men of the 2nd Duke of Cornwall's Light Infantry and the 2nd York & Lancaster effectively stalled the Egyptian advance with accurate long-range fire from their Martini-Henrys. A renewed Egyptian assault upon the British at Kassassin on 9 September was again halted by sustained long-range fire.

At the final battle of the conflict, Wolseley planned a night march across the desert to storm the formidable Egyptian defences at Tel el-Kebir. Arriving at dawn on 13 September, British troops, principally Highland regiments in the first assault, took the Egyptians by surprise and stormed the position. Despite some fierce hand-to-hand fighting the British, equipped with the Pattern 1876 Socket Bayonet, or 'lunger', with a reach of over 6ft, were able to overcome some initial stubborn Egyptian resistance.

The Martini-Henry was next to see service in the African continent during the Sudanese campaigns of 1884–85, first in the desert battles of Eastern Sudan and then during the unsuccessful Gordon Relief Expedition to Khartoum. Fighting the fanatical supporters of the Mahdi, known as Dervishes, the British encountered an enemy who was ready to give his life in a frantic charge. The terrain over which the British were forced to campaign allowed for concealment of large bodies of the enemy and at the battles of Tamai (13 March 1884), Abu Klea (17 January 1885) and Tofrek (22 March 1885) the British were surprised by a sudden onslaught from the enemy. To defend themselves against such a determined foe in such difficult terrain, British commanders such as General Sir Gerald Graham and Brigadier-General Herbert Stewart resorted to the use of the square formation; this was used not just only in combat but also on the line of march. Such a deployment meant that the British could not be outflanked, but also that the Martini-Henrys offered a wall of fire and steel against the Mahdist warriors.

'The Battle of Tofrek' by C.E. Fripp shows the 1st Berkshire in that battle of 22 March 1885. For its part in the action the regiment won the honour of being named The Princess Charlotte of Wales's (Royal Berkshire Regiment). In many of the Sudanese and Egyptian battles of 1884 and 1885 the ease of reloading of the Martini-Henry rifle, and thus the rate of fire, often made the difference between life and death. Of less reliability was the quality of the steel used to make the bayonets. (Courtesy of The Rifles (Berkshire and Wiltshire) Museum, Salisbury)

The issue of sand and dust entering the breech mechanism and causing jamming had first been noted in Egypt in 1882, but during the battles in the Sudan this issue became more prominent; the War Office had already established a special committee on cartridge jamming under Colonel Philip Smith in October 1885, but the Stephens Commission of 1887 took further evidence of complaints. Bennet Burleigh, the war correspondent of the *Daily Telegraph*, had his own Martini-Henry jam at Abu Klea. Smith took testimony not only from Lieutenant-Colonel the Hon. R.A.J. Talbot, who had commanded the Heavy Camel Regiment at Abu Klea, but also from non-commissioned officers and ordinary soldiers. Jamming, it was claimed, had occurred in between 25 per cent and 50 per cent of the rifles used. Smith and his colleagues concluded that although the effects of sand and dust had not helped, problems had also arisen from weak extractors, too heavy a charge, and overexcited soldiers. A solid cartridge and a better extractor, therefore, would solve some of the problems. The War Office committee also established that many of the troops were still armed with Mark I variants, whose inherent jamming problems had already been highlighted. Furthermore a number of men, although carrying later marks, were equipped with the Mark I cleaning rod, which was not long enough to clean the barrel properly, adding to problems of fouling (TNA SUPP 5/904).

The Stephens Commission concluded that heat and sand could not have been the only causes of jamming, or else it would have occurred more during earlier campaigns in South Africa, in which the issue had not been experienced to the same degree. *The Times* correspondent, writing on 23 April 1885, concluded that the thin cartridge rather than the sand was to blame. Major E. Gambier Parry, a former musketry instructor, served under Graham during the Suakin campaign of March 1885 and was present at the battle of Tofrek. He wrote a successful book of his experiences including his observations of the Martini-Henry:

> It not infrequently happened that the base of the cartridge was torn right off by the jaws of the extractor, when the rifle was at once rendered utterly useless. The sand and the temperature may have had a certain amount to do with the jamming, but the fault lay principally in the extractor of the rifle and the form of cartridge. The extractor

Lance-corporal of The Queen's Own Cameron Highlanders demonstrating the drill for 'charging bayonet' to receive an onrushing enemy, c. 1890–91. (Courtesy of the Victorian Military Society)

Firing the Martini-Henry

Firing the Martini-Henry Rifle and Cavalry Carbine is both a pleasure and a pain. A pleasure because it is both a privilege to do so and has allowed me to meet some fascinating individuals, but a pain when the recoil of the rifle first bangs into your nose!

Arguably, more has been written about the foibles of the Martini-Henry than any other British rifle. The overheating of the barrel, the excessive recoil and its tendency to jam have all been discussed as part of the explanation behind British defeats or near-disasters, from iSandlwana onwards. The barrel overheating issue was highlighted by troops who fought at Rorke's Drift and at the Sherpur cantonment, both of which were prolonged encounters over several hours, during which large numbers of cartridges were fired. In the case of Rorke's Drift this was in excess of 200 rounds per man.

However, these two battles were very much the exception to the rule of Victorian colonial conflict. For example, troops at Khambula fired an average of 33 rounds over a four-hour period and Abu Klea was over in little more than ten minutes. In both these cases, the few rounds fired would not have caused excessive heating of the barrels. I sincerely believe that this barrel heating has been overstressed by historians and commentators, based on the 'classic' examples, such as Sherpur, when cartridge expenditure was high and overheating of barrels expected. With this theory in mind, I fired half a dozen rounds in quick succession through both a Martini-Henry Rifle Mark II and Cavalry Carbine Mark I and found the barrels to be indeed warm, but not excessively so. Indeed, I found that the Martini-Henry barrels felt no warmer than a 12-bore shotgun would be after firing 20 or so cartridges in a matter of a few minutes. The barrels of the two Martini-Henrys were certainly not too hot to touch and would certainly not have stopped me firing several more rounds through the barrels.

The recoil was surprising in two ways. First, it was in no way as strong as I expected it to be and again, in terms of the recoil to my shoulder, I felt it was no more than firing a 12-bore shotgun. Second, however, the recoil also manifested itself in a tendency for the barrel to spring upwards on firing. This resulted, initially, in a tendency to fire high of the target, but also for the block of the rifle to rise up and hit my nose. This was painful and slightly shocking at first, but I was able to compensate for this action over time and improved both my accuracy and lessened the damage to my nose!

Firing both the rifle and carbine with black-powder loads generated a great deal of smoke and, on the still day that I fired the weapons, the smoke hung in the air for minutes after. I can only imagine how a battlefield must have been obscured by the smoke from several hundred Martinis firing at once. The noise too from just one rifle was incredibly loud and again, battlefield conditions must have produced deafness in troops, even if only temporarily.

Jamming of spent cartridge cases was not a problem and some myths concerning the jamming were again disproved during my shooting session. Of course jamming first came to light in the Swinburne-Henry carbine, which, as Redvers Buller wrote, was so notorious. For some commentators this was carried over to the Martini-Henry carbine, but of course the actions of these two weapons were completely different and it is unfair to label the Martini-Henry carbine with the faults of the Swinburne. However, there are many examples quoted of Martini-Henry rifles jamming, particularly in the campaigns of Egyptian and the Sudan when sand is reported to have invaded the block mechanism or cartridge cases tore in the barrel. In my limited experience, but after the discussion with others who have fired the Martini-Henry many times, jamming is rare, but the historical descriptions of how to unjam seem to be inaccurate. For example, there is no way in which the point of a knife could be inserted into the barrel to free the cartridge case for there is simply insufficient room and even fingers might not be successful. It was clear to me that if a jam did occur the quickest, most efficient way to expel the cartridge case is to use the cleaning rod, perhaps with the jag attached, and to poke this down the barrel. The offending case then simply drops out and this takes seconds to achieve.

My overwhelming feeling from having both fired the Martini-Henry rifle and carbine was how easy both were to use. Within firing 20 rounds I was consistently able to hit a target at 100yd. Loading was straightforward and quick to achieve. I also found the removal of spent cartridges to be much easier than I thought it to be. Overall, I was pleasantly surprised to find both weapons so, to use a modern term, 'user friendly' and I believe that the 'Soldiers of the Queen' found their own Martinis just the same. It has been modern writers who have over-emphasised the weapon's apparent failings at the expense of its positive features.

ABOVE Firing the Martini-Henry Rifle Mark II, illustrating the amount of smoke produced by black-powder cartridges. (Author)

ought certainly to be improved upon if this is to continue [as] the arm of the services; and a drawn copper cartridge-case, unduplicated, should take the place of the present one. (Gambier Parry 1886: 195)

While this debate carried on, the soldiers themselves took matters into their own hands. Weapons were cleaned more frequently and the stopping-power of the cartridge was enhanced against the sheer velocity of the Dervish charge by nicking the bullets, which increased their destructive power upon impact with bone and cartilage and effectively transformed them into 'dum-dum' bullets. The troops soon learnt that even a Martini-Henry round to the body would not necessarily stop the enemy and that to fire low at least immobilized them. Furthermore, with controversy surrounding the cartridge, Wolseley, commanding the Gordon Relief Expedition, demanded in January 1885 that rolled brass should replace the sheet brass formerly used.[4] The British Government hastily agreed, but the new cartridges were supplied too late for use in the campaigns of 1885.

However, it was not just jamming and concern over the cartridges that caused controversy during the Sudanese campaign. The determination of the enemy to close on the British resulted in much hand-to-hand fighting and at both the battles of Tamaai and Abu Klea, the Dervish forces broke into the British squares. On both occasions, errors by individuals or by units moving out of position can explain the near-reversals for the British, and at no time have these setbacks been attributed to the jamming of the Martini-Henry. Yet the resultant fierce close combat revealed that the steel used to make the Pattern 1876 Socket Bayonet was frequently faulty. The result was bayonets that bent or twisted on impact with bone, making retrieval difficult. At Abu Klea bayonets were also found to have been bent when camels rolled or fell onto them. At Abu Klea, Gilligan of the 2nd Life Guards reported that his bayonet had twisted like a corkscrew as he had plunged it into an enemy (Bickley n.d.: 50). Again, Gambier Parry felt compelled to comment: 'A jammed rifle may be of use to the man who can go in with bayonet, but how about a rifle with a bent bayonet in front of the muzzle? The first is bad enough, but in the latter case the weapon is rendered utterly useless' (Gambier Parry 1886: 196). The issue of faulty steel was even raised in Parliament, which concluded its debate with the firm assurance that new bayonets would be issued, as indeed they were in the form of the Pattern 1888 Lee-Metford Bayonet.

Although the campaigns in the Sudan of 1884–85 were characterized by the use of the square formation, the British did achieve one significant victory against Mahdist forces at the battle of Kirbekan (10 February 1885) at which the range and killing power of the Martini-Henry was ably demonstrated. The British, under the command of Major-General William Earle (1833–85), encountered a significant enemy force in rocky ground. Rather than wait to be attacked, Earle sent men of the 1st Black

---

4   Initially, cartridges were manufactured of rolled brass foil with an iron rim, but after it was discovered that the rolled-foil cartridges were prone to jamming as the barrel heated up, production was switched to the drawn-brass style now commonly used for the manufacture of small-arms ammunition

Watch and 1st South Staffordshire on a flanking movement to attack the Dervishes in the rear, while the remainder of his force edged towards the enemy position. Attacking in open order, the British were able to shoot down the counterattacking Dervishes before they could engage with the British. Accurate and concentrated Martini-Henry volley fire achieved a notable British victory, although Earle himself was killed. Similarly, although surprised, British and Indian troops (the Indian forces armed with the Snider-Enfield) were successful at the battle of Tofrek. A combination of fire discipline, the ability to rapidly form a square and the rapid fire of the Martini-Henry allowed the British to snatch victory from almost certain defeat.

BURMA

The Martini-Henry did see service in Burma, but this was somewhat limited, for most of the fighting was undertaken by the Indian Army, armed with the Snider-Enfield rifle. Indeed as the Martini-Henry was supplied to the Indian Army, serving throughout India and on the North West Frontier, it was policy for the remaining serviceable Snider-Enfields to be sent to troops and police serving in Burma. Thus the Snider-Enfield remained in service in Burma far longer than in any other conflict zone of the empire.

British front-line troops, the 1st Royal Welsh Fusiliers and the 2nd Royal Hampshire, did see action during the 3rd Anglo-Burmese War (1885–89). The only significant battle of this war was at Minhla on 17 November 1885. After a bombardment from British artillery, the Burmese stockade was stormed. Both the Martini-Henry and Snider-Enfield saw action, as British and Indian troops cleared and burned the town. After this engagement, the British entered Mandalay and deposed the Burmese king, Thibaw. The war now degenerated into one of skirmish and ambush as the Burmese resistance fighters, or *dacoits*, retreated into the jungle from where attacks were launched not only at the imperial troops but also at the civil population who were forced to supply the *dacoits*. The remaining years of the war were a frustrating game of 'cat and mouse' in which the British and Indian forces found it difficult to operate in the jungle terrain. Resistance was finally brought under control as the number of *dacoits* dwindled. Even so, the British were forced to maintain a substantial military presence in the country for a number of years and, even into the 1890s, significant military expeditions had to be launched against isolated pockets of resistance.

By the end of the 1880s the Martini-Henry had seen service across Africa and had acquitted itself well in Afghanistan and across the empire. Yet the introduction of the Lee-Metford magazine rifle in 1888 marked the demise of the Martini-Henry in front-line use by the British Army. However, the Martini-Henry had many years of distinguished service still ahead of it in the colonial armies of the British Empire.

IMPACT

Icon of the height of Empire

On 19 August 1874 as the Martini-Henry rifle entered British service, *The Times* proclaimed it 'the most magnificent weapon ever placed in the hands of a soldier'. The historian Daniel Headrick has described the Martini-Henry as 'the first really satisfactory rifle of the new generation' (Headrick 1981: 98). The rifle had the heaviest bullet, the lowest trajectory and the highest muzzle velocity of any rifle then in service in the world. It seems that it could have been specifically designed for use against the 'savage foes' between 1879 and 1889, rather than as a result of the urgent need to compete with the rifles of Britain's European rivals.

Contemporaries extolled the merits of the Martini-Henry. Rudyard Kipling, perhaps the ultimate literary chronicler of the Victorian soldier, wrote of the Martini-Henry in two of his poems. In *'The Young British Soldier' he wrote:*

> When 'arf of your bullets fly wide in the ditch,
> Don't call your Martini a cross-eyed old bitch;
> She's human as you are – yoo treat her as sich,
> An' she'll fight for the young British soldier. (Kipling 1990: 337)

The rifle is also mentioned in Kipling's poem, *'Fuzzy Wuzzy'*, set in the Eastern Sudan:

> We sloshed you with Martinis, an' it wasn't 'ardly fair;
> But for all the odds agin' you, Fuzzy-Wuz, you broke the square.
> (Kipling 1990: 445)

The Martini-Henry featured in Kipling's short story *The Man Who Would Be King* (1888) and also in 'The Black Jack' from *Soldiers Three and Other Stories* (1888). Other writers of the period also mention the Martini-Henry. These include Bram Stoker in his work of 1895, *The Watter's Mou*, O. Henry in his short story 'The Admiral' from *Cabbages and Kings* (1896), and Joseph Conrad in his infamous and atmospheric *Heart of Darkness* (1902). The Australian author William Hughes Willshire wrote, in his work *The Land of the Dawning*, 'the

'The Storming of the Heights of Dargai' by Vereker M. Hamilton. Note in the foreground the soldier of the 1/3rd Gurkhas is holding a Martini-Henry rifle, while the men of the 1st Gordon Highlanders are armed with the new Lee-Metford rifle. (Gregory Fremont-Barnes)

Martini-Henry carbines at the critical moment were talking English in the silent majesty of these eternal rocks' (quoted in Beckett, forthcoming). The rifle's cultural significance can be further emphasised by the fact that a celebrated New Zealand-bred mare, '*Martini-Henry*', won both the Victoria Derby and the Melbourne Cup in 1883.

However, the Martini-Henry was not to remain in British front-line service for long. Although there had been issues of jamming, which General Buller, writing after the failed Gordon Relief Expedition, claimed had led to a mistrust of the Martini amongst British troops, this was not to be the reason for the Martini's front-line demise. The Martini-Henry became a casualty of technical innovation, which would see the British develop a magazine-fed rifle as its replacement.

The Martini-Henry had proved itself to be a 'soldier-proof' weapon and this, combined with its relatively easy manufacture and its ability to be modified successfully, resulted in the .303in Martini-Metford and Martini-Enfield variants. These rifles benefited from the introduction of a smokeless propellant called nitrocellulose that burned hotter and faster than black powder, resulting in higher pressure and higher velocity. However, the desire for a superior weapon, possessing a magazine from which eight or ten cartridges could be accessed, had become more widespread in the 1880s, as a result of technological advancements in Europe and America. As a result of the deliberations of the War Office Committee on Martini-Henry Rifles and Ammunition, a new Small Arms Committee had been formed in February 1883 under the chairmanship of Philip Smith, to continue the examination of a number of experimental magazine rifles. Several futile attempts were made to try to convert the Martini into a magazine-fed rifle, the Owen-Jones slide-action rifle being just one example. However, the Martini's falling-block action made conversion both extremely difficult and expensive and it soon became evident that a new rifle would have to be considered. A pattern was approved in October 1885, and issued for trials in June 1886. Ultimately, the .303in Lee-Metford, a combination of the bolt-action system of the

Boer burghers (leaders) from the Orange Free State in 1899. The young man on the far right is holding a Martini-Henry rifle, while his comrades all hold Mauser rifles. (Courtesy of Ian Knight)

Scottish-born American inventor James Paris Lee and the rifling of the English engineer William Ellis Metford, went into production in December 1888. After major manufacturing issues were encountered, an announcement that the Lee-Metford was to enter British service was only made a year later, in December 1889.

This news was not to prompt the immediate demise of the Martini-Henry. The adoption of the Lee-Metford provoked as much controversy as the Martini-Henry had. With 37 more components than the Martini-Henry (which had 19 parts in the breech block, plus barrel, stock and fittings for the bayonet), the Lee-Metford required 620 more processes to manufacture, and it took 559 more workmen and 30,186 more man-hours to produce 1,000 rifles (HCPP 1890–91 (63)). These extra hours simply meant that the rate of entry of the replacement weapon into service was much delayed and partly explains why the Martini-Henry remained in service for so many additional years.

Ever since the Indian Uprising of 1857, it had been the policy of both the Indian and British Governments to arm Indian troops with weapons that had been discontinued in service with British forces. Hence in the 2nd Anglo-Afghan War Indian Army troops were armed with the Snider-Enfield, as they were in the Sudan in 1885. Indeed at the battle of Tofrek, volley fire from the Snider-Enfield had a significant impact at a crucial moment in the battle. With the introduction of the Lee-Metford it was thought that the Indian Army, as well as troops serving in other colonial forces such as Egypt and Sudan, would be issued with the Martini-Henry. Of course the matter was far more complicated than a simple handover, and indeed the process had already begun. As early as 1885 the British Government had agreed that the Martini-Henry should be supplied to the Indian Army. General Allen B. Johnson, the Military Secretary to the India Office, had written to the Indian Government on 2 September 1885, 'we are putting forward a demand for 94,000 rifles and 25,250 carbines of the Martini-Henry pattern with the object of implementing the armament of the entire Native army with the best weapons available and placing them in this respect on an equal footing with the British troops' (TNA Coll. 267/1).

However, the introduction of the Martini-Metford, and later the Martini-Enfield, resulted in delays and confusion regarding the supply of new Martinis to the Indian Army. By May 1886 only 40,000 Martini-Henry rifles and 5,500 carbines had been supplied and the rest of the order had been cancelled, awaiting the introduction of the Martini-Enfield. Further confusion resulted from the news of the Lee-Metford magazine rifle entering British service. The Viceroy of India, writing to the War Office in August 1887, questioned whether it was likely that such weapons would be issued to India (TNA Coll. 267/14). With production delays and difficulties in England, the issue of the Lee-Metford to British front-line troops became problematic and it was soon clear that the Indian Army could not expect an early issue of the magazine rifles.

With stocks of Snider-Enfield and Martini-Henry rifles dangerously low and with the difficulty of converting the Martini-Henry barrel to .303in calibre in India, the Indian Government was forced to order supplies of Martini-Henry rifles and carbines from Britain; this order was placed in August 1890. A total of 75,000 rifles and 30,000 carbines were duly dispatched, although the War Office did admit that the 'Marks II and III are part worn, but serviceable arms; Mark IV are new' (TNA Coll. 267/23B). Thus as British and Indian troops fought alongside each other in the numerous campaigns in the North West Frontier in the 1890s, the British were armed with the Lee-Metford, while the Indian troops carried into battle the Martini-Henry. Famously at the battle of Dargai Heights (20 October 1897) during the Tirah campaign the 1st Gordon Highlanders and 1/3rd Gurkhas who took part in the successful assault were armed with Lee-Metfords and Martini-Henry rifles respectively. It would not be until the turn of the century that, with production difficulties eased and British troops equipped, the Indian Army would be issued with a magazine rifle.

Men of the 12th Sudanese Battalion armed with Mark II and Mark III rifles await the Dervish attack, 2 September 1898. The slower reloading and single-shot nature of the Martini-Henry rifle, as used by the Sudanese troops, meant that the attacking Dervishes were able to advance closer to the Sudanese position than they were able to against the British troops armed with the Lee-Enfield magazine rifle. (National Army Museum)

Other colonial forces continued to use the Martini-Henry long after it had left British front-line service. Some Australian troops used Martini-Henrys during the 2nd Anglo-Boer War (1899–1902) and Martinis were issued to African troops guarding the British 'blockhouses' that eventually snaked across the South African veldt. Boers too, when their beloved Mausers were in short supply, could be found using Martinis against the British. Well into the 1890s the governments of such diverse colonies as Canada and Jamaica were still placing orders for Martini weapons (Temple & Skennerton 1989: 395). The photographs that survive from Queen Victoria's Diamond Jubilee celebrations of 1897, at which military contingents from all over the Empire took part in a Royal march-past, show a mixed collection of Martini weapons still in service. The Martini was still in use with The King's African Rifles well into the 1900s.

The Egyptian and Sudanese battalions present alongside British troops at the battle of Omdurman (2 September 1898) were armed with Martini-Henry rifles. While the British, equipped with Lee-Metfords, opened fire at the advancing Dervishes at 2,000yd and stopped the enemy at 800yd, Sudanese troops began firing at a distance of 1,000yd and stopped the Dervishes 500yd from their position (Haythornthwaite 1997: 37); such was the superior velocity, range and rate of fire of the Lee-Metford. Indeed, fitted as it was with a long-range, or volley, sight on the left side of the body, the Lee-Metford could, theoretically, be aimed at targets at ranges in excess of 3,000yd. As no human target would be visible at such distances, the sight could be used to aim at massed targets and its success at Omdurman is evidence of the Lee-Metford's superiority over the Martini-Henry.

The battle of Omdurman can be viewed as a triumph of the industrial and technological strength possessed by the British Empire over its enemies at that time, with the Lee-Metford as the epitome of this. For the loss of just 48 officers and men (and a large proportion of these had been lost in the foolhardy and unnecessary charge of the 21st Lancers) and 382 wounded, this force inflicted casualties amounting to nearly 11,000 fatalities and at least 16,000 wounded upon the Mahdist army of roughly 50,000 men. The battle can also be seen as a triumph of empire, with British, Sudanese and Egyptian troops serving alongside each other. It is also fitting to recognize that the Martini-Henry, in the hands of colonial units, had still been able to make a significant contribution to the final victory.

The rifle-volunteer movement in Britain was not fully equipped with the Martini-Henry until 1885, and did not begin to receive the Lee-Metford until 1895. The Martini, frequently the carbine, became the weapon of choice for cadet forces across Britain, and remained so well into the 20th century. Many of the future soldiers and officers of World War I, and even World War II, had first learnt to shoot using a Martini-Henry either at school or at shooting clubs, often attached to large enterprises such as collieries. Christ College in Brecon was typical of many of the cadet corps in Britain that were issued with the Martini-Henry. The weapon first arrived at the school in the late 1880s and was used by the students for drill three times a week; a visit to the firing range was a monthly treat. In 1897 the school received replacement Martini-Metford carbines and these were to be used by the boys until after World War I. Territorial Army units could occasionally be seen using the Martini until 1910 and the artist Richard Caton Woodville Jr (1856–1927), in his 1908 *Territorial Army Album*, painted a Martini Artillery Carbine. The Royal Irish Constabulary still had Martini carbines in the 1920s, as did the IRA.

The Martini-Henry could occasionally be found in the hands of Britain's foes. Both the Zulus at iSandlwana and the Afghans at Maiwand captured substantial numbers of Martini-Henry rifles. In the case of the Zulus these were rather ineffectually used against the British at both

The North West Frontier, 1898 (opposite)

This plate illustrates a scene that typically took place during the Tirah campaign of 1897–98. After the British success at the battle of Dargai Heights (20 October 1897), the campaign focused on depriving the rebellious Afridi and Orakzai tribesmen of food and shelter by burning crops and villages, and thus limiting their ability to offer resistance. During these operations it was common for British and Indian troops to be sniped at by the tribesmen, who often sought cover behind rocks and fired down upon the 'invaders' who were marching in the valley below. The British commanders reacted to such fire by sending Indian and Gurkha troops up the mountain sides, so as to outflank the snipers, whilst the British troops, armed with the Lee-Metford rifle, returned fire and tried to 'pin down' the enemy. Frequently, the tribesmen retreated before the Indian forces could engage with them.

The scene illustrated shows one Afridi tribesmen, armed with a captured Martini-Henry rifle, loading his prize as he readies to fire down upon the advancing column of troops from the 15th and 36th Sikhs and the 1st Northamptonshire in the valley below. The tribesman has positioned spare cartridges near at hand so as to be able to reload quickly. The men of the Afridi and Orakzai tribes were renowned marksmen who valued the range and accuracy of the Martini-Henry rifle, so much so that 'Khyber Pass' copies of the Martini-Henry were made in the region well into the 20th century and were used against Soviet, British and American troops in more recent conflicts. In the background, two tribesmen, armed with the long-barrelled traditional jezail rifles, are shown firing down upon the column.

A Martini-Henry carbine, probably originating from the 'factories' of the North West Frontier, showing poor finishing around the trigger and 'ENFIELD' engraved upside down – a 'Khyber Pass Copy'. (Author)

Khambula and Ulundi. The Afghans were better able to use their prizes and with its ease of use, and firepower, the Martini-Henry rifle remained a popular weapon among the hill tribes of the North West Frontier.

Following a surprise attack at Medina Creek during the 1894 Gambia campaign, some 60 officers and men of the Naval Brigade were killed and wounded; their Martini-Henrys were captured by the Mandingo tribesmen who defeated them. Soon afterwards, on 25 February 1894, the British skirmished with the enemy and discovered that the captured Martinis were now being used against them. One of the officers recorded:

> Five miles in rear was Fort St. Mary, held by a small party of bluejackets, and in front was an unknown number of Mandingoes, estimated according to some accounts at as many as two thousand, flushed with their repulse of the Naval Brigade. About 5.30 next morning a sentry on the right gave the alarm, and we could just make out in the dim light two parties of men, each numbering about a hundred, rushing towards our right flank, having plainly been attempting to steal round our rear… In a few seconds every man was in his place, and our right section poured in a volley which made them disappear in to the bushes, while still some two hundred yards away from us. Almost immediately a heavy fire broke out in front on our left flank, and the bushes seemed alive with men. Lying down we fired volleys by sections into the bush wherever the flashes of their guns appeared thickest. For more than half an hour the fire was very heavy, slugs were flying about too thick to be quite pleasant, and the unmistakeable whiz of Martini bullets was to be heard just over-head, telling us that some of the rifles lost by the Naval Brigade were being used against us. (Quoted in Blumberg & Field 1934: 300)

Fortunately for the British the Mandingoes, as with many of the Zulus before them, seemed unable to understand the importance of adjusting the sights, as acknowledged by a British officer present: 'A number of empty Martini-Henry cartridge cases were found on the field, showing that several of the rifles lost at Medina Creek were used against us, but the Mandingoes luckily did not know how to use them, and fired too high' (Blumberg & Field 1934: 301).

Whether as a weapon captured from British or Indian troops or as a 'reproduction', the Martini-Henry has been, until relatively recently, a common enough sight in the mountains of the Hindu Kush. As late as the 1940s, local craftsmen were reproducing 'Martini-Henry' rifles and carbines in village workshops and blacksmiths' shops across the region. Indeed, the Martini-Henry was one of the most prolifically copied weapons, although today it has been replaced by the AK-47. One of the peculiarities of these so-called 'Khyber Pass Martinis' or 'Pass-made rifles' is that village gunsmiths even tried to copy, generally with limited success, the stampings and markings from their original source weapon. Errors in spelling, for example the 'N' in 'ENFIELD' stamped backwards, or words and markings upside down, are common mistakes and make the weapon easily identifiable as a 'Khyber Pass Copy'. Likewise, implausible date stamps, such as '1919' appearing on a Mark II rifle, are frequently seen. Usually the quality of metallurgy, the wood of the stock and the screws used on the trigger are all evident clues as to the weapon's providence. Unlike genuine British-made Martini-Henrys these copies are not very collectable, and sell for a fraction of the price. A word of caution: while serviceable Martini-Henrys can be fired today, if you happen to own such a copy do not consider firing the weapon, as it could blow up in your face.

Martini-Henry rifles and carbines have appeared in the most unlikely places and it seems clear that there must have been a healthy 'second-hand' market for these weapons, whether legal or not. For example, in 1888 the Ndebele chief Lobengula received 1,000 Martini-Henry rifles from the Rudd Mining Company as the price for granting mining concessions. These weapons were used in 1896 by the Ndebele against the British South African Company. The Khama were similarly supplied with Martinis, again for mining concessions, by the Bechuanaland Exploration Company. The Khama even wrote a Kgatla praise poem to celebrate the use of the Martini against the Boers. The Martini-Henry has also been a favoured weapon of Bedouin tribesmen, and it is difficult to imagine how the rifle found its way to such grateful users. Like the tribesmen of the North West Frontier, the Bedouin might simply have copied the British design or acquired Trade patterns.

Temple and Skennerton have claimed that there is reason to believe that standard Martini Service patterns, including the Martini-Henry rifle, were re-issued for training purposes during the early years of World War I, when .303in magazine rifles were in short supply. These authors state that a combination of wartime censorship and a lack of interest after the war ended has meant that this aspect of Martini-Henry service is poorly documented and details of the numbers and variants used are not readily available (Temple & Skennerton 1995: 594). The British even found a use for the solid-case Boxer-Henry cartridge during the early years of World War I – as the basis for incendiary bullets against raiding Zeppelins in 1915.

The longevity of the Martini-Henry, in use both at home among cadet and Volunteer units and in active service by colonial forces, is remarkable. The weapon was easy to use and clean, was sturdy and dependable. The Martini-Henry's impact upon the history of military arms was hugely significant and long lasting. The fact that it was prized and copied by Britain's foes is testimony to its success.

CONCLUSION

Although in poor condition, this photograph shows a rare image of a black African soldier named Jim, serving during the 2nd Anglo-Boer War (1899–1902). He holds a Francotte-action 'improved' Martini made by Westley Richards for the South African Government. Many black troops were used by the British to serve as blockhouse guards in the chain of fortified posts built to hamper the free movement of Boer commandos. (Courtesy of Edward Garcia, Soldiers of the Queen website)

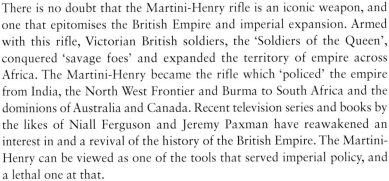

There is no doubt that the Martini-Henry rifle is an iconic weapon, and one that epitomises the British Empire and imperial expansion. Armed with this rifle, Victorian British soldiers, the 'Soldiers of the Queen', conquered 'savage foes' and expanded the territory of empire across Africa. The Martini-Henry became the rifle which 'policed' the empire from India, the North West Frontier and Burma to South Africa and the dominions of Australia and Canada. Recent television series and books by the likes of Niall Ferguson and Jeremy Paxman have reawakened an interest in and a revival of the history of the British Empire. The Martini-Henry can be viewed as one of the tools that served imperial policy, and a lethal one at that.

Yet, despite a few notable Victorian exceptions, the position of the Martini-Henry as a cultural icon is fundamentally a 20th- and 21st-century development. It has been through the medium of film, specifically the 1964 motion picture *Zulu*, that the Martini-Henry, and all that it epitomises, has come to be known to a wider audience (*Zulu* was ranked eighth in a website poll for Channel Four's '100 Greatest War Movies' programme in 2005). Appearances in such other films as *The Man Who Would Be King* (1975), *Zulu Dawn* (1979), *The Ghost and the Darkness* (1996), in which a Mark III plays a very prominent part, *The Four Feathers* (2002) and the New Zealand film *Tracker* (2009) have, arguably, made the Martini-Henry one of the most instantly recognizable of all firearms.

It could also be argued that the film *Zulu* has spawned two separate industries. First, the publishing industry has been, and continues to be, enthusiastic in producing history books on the subject of the Anglo-Zulu War, frequently at the expense of other, equally fascinating, Victorian campaigns. Indeed, since the year 2000 over 20 titles have been published on the Anglo-

Zulu War in which, of course, the Martini-Henry played such a prominent part. Second, Martini-Henrys have become highly desirable collector's pieces. Prices in excess of £1,500 a piece are not uncommon and one antiques dealer was quoted in *the Independent newspaper* (8 June 2008), as saying, 'The Martini-Henry is a very, very collectable gun and this is (almost) entirely due to Michael Caine and the film *Zulu*.' Similarly, spent bullets, real or not, from Anglo-Zulu War battle sites trade on internet auction sites for sums of around £100. Martini-Henry rifles and carbines have, in recent years, entered both Britain and the United States with troops returning from Afghanistan. There was considerable media interest in 2008 when two Martinis, captured from Taliban insurgents in Afghanistan, appeared in a Brighton antique shop. Both rifles were believed to have been taken originally from the bodies of British troops killed in Afghanistan in 1880. Similarly, as already discussed, many Khyber Pass copies have been brought back by returning British and American troops.

The weapon's cultural impact has materialized itself in some unusual ways. For example, between 2001 and 2006, there was a Cardiff-based group, 'The Martini Henry Rifles', which was characterized both as an 'alternative new wave punk' and as a 'noise-punk' band. The internet is home to numerous websites that focus solely on the Martini-Henry.

It is easy to consider the Martini-Henry a problematic weapon. However, defects resulted mostly from the Boxer-Henry cartridge rather than the weapon itself, and these faults did not lead materially to British military failures. The overheating of the barrel and the sometimes excessive recoil of the rifle should not be considered unusual for weapons of the period. Indeed the overheating issue should not be exaggerated. Only in engagements such as Rorke's Drift and Sherpur was the rifle fired excessively and it was in these battles that the overheating of barrels was stressed by the combatants. At other times, the slow, steady fire of British troops trained in such disciplines meant that overheating was not significant. Defeats such as those at iSandlwana and Maiwand can be attributed to poor leadership, and an underestimation of opponents' capabilities, rather than any inherent shortcomings of the Martini-Henry rifle.

While the monarch, politicians, economists and generals may have been the driving forces behind imperial expansion, it was the 'Soldiers of the Queen' who ensured that the policies were carried out. Armed with the robust and easy-to-use Martini-Henry rifle, these British troops were equipped with a weapon that served them well and very rarely let them down. The longevity of the weapon in the hands of colonial forces, Volunteer reserves, cadet units and Afghan tribesmen is testimony to the strength of the basic design. There is no doubt that the Martini-Henry rifle is an important part of British military history.

A fine study of an NCO of a unit believed to be The King's African Rifles taken in East Africa in about 1905. He wears four campaign medals, the first of which is the Central African Medal, with bar, 'Central Africa 1894–98', earned as a member of The Central African Rifles. He is armed with a Martini-Enfield Rifle Mark I. (Courtesy of Edward Garcia, Soldiers of the Queen website)

BIBLIOGRAPHY

Primary sources

Argyll and Sutherland Highlanders Museum
Diary of 2nd Lieutenant R. Wolrige Gordon, Grenadier Guards, ASHM N-C91. GOR.W

Killie Campbell Collection, University of KwaZulu-Natal
Symons Papers

Leicestershire Record Office
Record Book of the Seventeenth, or Leicestershire Regiment of Infantry. 22D63/32 1878–81

National Army Museum
Diary of Private J.A. Facer, 30th Regiment, Acc. No. 8301/131

Royal Green Jackets Museum
Zulu War Journal of Corporal John Hargreaves, 3/60th Rifles, Lib. RGJ, D.37

The National Archives, UK
British Library, Asia, Pacific and Africa Collections, Collection 267: Small Arms and Ammunition, IOR/L/MIL/7/11964–12060 (1885–1932):
Coll. 267/1: Snider rifles and ammunition: demands cancelled, IOR/L/MIL/7/11964 (1885)
Coll. 267/14: Supply of new pattern magazine rifles to British troops in India, IOR/L/MIL/7/11979 (1887–88)
Coll. 267/23B: Martini-Henry rifles: demand for 75,000 .45 rifles and 30,000 carbines, IOR/L/MIL/7/11990 (1890)
Records created or inherited by the Ministry of Supply and successors, the Ordnance Board, and related bodies (1664–1988):
SUPP 5/904: Special Committee on Small Arms, Report on Jamming of Cartridges in Martini-Henry Rifles in Egypt (1885–86)
War Office: Reports, Memoranda and Papers (O and A Series) (1853–1969):
Musketry Instruction Manual (1874)
Reports on Breech-loading Arms by a Special Sub-committee of the Ordnance Select Committee (1868)

House of Commons parliamentary papers
1890–91 (63) *Army Rifles*

Secondary sources
Ashe, Major & Wyatt-Edgell, Captain (1880). *The Story of the Zulu Campaign.* London: Sampson and Low
Asher, M. (2005). *Khartoum – The Ultimate Imperial Adventure.* London: Viking

Black, J. (2007). *Tools of War: The Weapons that Changed the World*.
    London: Quercus
Black, J. (2009). *War in the Nineteenth Century 1800–1914*.
    London: Polity
Blumberg, General Sir H.E. & Field, Colonel C. (1934). *A Record of
    The Royal Marines 1837–1914*. Devonport: Swift & Co
Callwell, Colonel C.E. (1896). *Small Wars: Their Principles and Practice*.
    London: HMSO
Curling, H. (2001). *The Curling Letters of the Zulu War*,
    ed. A. Greaves & B. Best. Barnsley: Pen & Sword
David, S. (2004). *Zulu*. London: Viking
Duckers, P. (2005). *British Military Rifles 1800–2000*. Princes
    Risborough: Shire Publications
Emery, F. (1983). *The Red Soldier: The Zulu War of 1879*.
    Johannesburg: Jonathan Ball
Featherstone, D. (1978). *Weapons and Equipment of the Victorian
    Soldier*. Poole: Blandford Press
Gambier Parry, Major E. (1886). *Suakin 1885: A Sketch of the
    Campaign*. London: John Murray
Gon, P. (1979). *The Road to Isandlwana*. Johannesburg: A.D. Donker
Greaves, A. (2005). *Crossing the Buffalo: The Zulu War of 1879*.
    London: Weidenfeld & Nicolson
Guy, J.J. (1971). '*A Note on Firearms in the Zulu Kingdom with Special
    Reference to the Anglo-Zulu War of 1879*' in *The Journal of
    African History*, Vol. 12, No. 4: 567–70
Haythornthwaite, P. (1997). *The Colonial Wars Source Book*.
    London: Arms & Armour Press
Headrick, D. (1981). *Tools of Empire: Technology and European
    Imperialism in the Nineteenth Century*. New York, NY: Oxford
    University Press
Headrick, D. (2010). *Power over Peoples: Technology, Environment and
    Western Imperialism, 1400 to the Present*.
    Princeton, NJ: Princeton University Press
Hope, R. (1997). *The Zulu War and the 80th Regiment of Foot*.
    London: Churnet Valley Books
Hope, R. (2007). *A Staffordshire Regiment in the Zulu & Sekukuni
    Campaigns*. London: Churnet Valley Books
Keown-Boyd, H. (1986). *A Good Dusting: The Sudan Campaigns
    1883–1899*. London: Leo Cooper.
Kipling, R. (1990). *The Complete Verse*. London: Kyle Cathie
Knight, I. (1991). Elite 32: *British Forces in Zululand 1879*.
    London: Osprey Publishing
Knight, I. (1993). *Nothing Remains But to Fight: The Defence of
    Rorke's Drift, 1879*. London: Greenhill Books
Knight I. (2002). '"*Old Steady Shots*": *The Martini-Henry Rifle, Rates
    of Fire and Effectiveness in the Anglo Zulu War*' in *The Journal
    of the Anglo-Zulu War Historical Society*, XI: 1–8
Knight, I. (2003). *The National Army Museum Book of the Zulu War*.
    London: Sidgwick & Jackson

Knight, I. (2010). *Zulu Rising: The Epic Story of Isandlwana and Rorke's Drift.* London: Macmillan

Knight, I. & Castle, I. (1994). *Fearful Hard Times: The Siege and Relief of Eshowe 1879.* London: Greenhill Books

Knight, I. & Castle, I. (2004). *Zulu War.* Oxford: Osprey

Laband, J. (1985). *Fight Us in the Open.* Johannesburg: Jonathan Ball

Laband, J. (1995). *Rope of Sand: the Rise and Fall of the Zulu Kingdom in the Nineteenth Century.* Johannesburg: Jonathan Ball

Laband, J. & Knight, I. (1996). *The War Correspondents: The Anglo-Zulu War.* Stroud: Sutton Publishing

Lewis, D. (1996). *Martini-Henry .450 Rifles & Carbines.* Tucson, AZ: Excalibur Publications

Manning, S. (2009). *Soldiers of the Queen: Colonial Conflict in the Words of Those that Fought.* Stroud: Spellmount

Marshall, W.P.P. (1871). 'The Martini Rifle and the Westley Richards Rifle' in *Engineering,* 27 April 1871

Miller, H.P. (2010). *A Guide to the Queen's Sixty OR Martini-Henry and Snider Rifles and How to Use Them.* Whitefish, MT: Kessinger Legacy Reprint. Originally published 1881

Moodie, D., ed. (1886). *John Dunn, Cetywayo and the Three Generals.* Pietermaritzburg: Natal Print and Publishing Company

Morris, D. (1965). *The Washing of the Spears.* New York, NY: Simon & Schuster

Myatt, F. (1970). *The March to Magdala: The Abyssinian War 1868.* London: Leo Cooper

Pridham, Major C. (1945). *Superiority of Fire: A Short History of Rifles and Machine-Guns.* London: Hutchinson

Prior, M. (1912). *Campaigns of a War Correspondent.* London: Edward Arnold

Raugh Jr, H. (2004). *The Victorian at War, 1815–1914: An Encyclopedia of British Military History.* Oxford: Clio

Robson, B. (2003). *The Road to Kabul: The Second Afghan War, 1878–1881.* Staplehurst: Spellmount

Scarlata, P. (2004). 'The British Martini-Henry Rifle' in *Shotgun News,* 6 December 2004: 36–40

School of Musketry (1873). *Trajectory Etc. of the Martini-Henry Rifle.* Hythe: School of Musketry

Skennerton, I. (2002). *.450 & .303 Martini Rifles and Carbines, Small Arms Identification Series No. 15,* Labrador: I. Skennerton

Smith-Dorrien, General Sir H. (1925). *Memories of 48 Years' Service.* London: John Murray

Snook, Lieutenant Colonel M. (2010). *Go Strong into the Desert: The Mahdist Uprising in Sudan 1881–5.* Nottingham: Perry Miniatures

Spiers, E. (1992). *The Late Victorian Army, 1868–1902.* Manchester: Manchester University Press

Spiers, E. (1998). *Sudan: The Reconquest Reappraised.* London: Frank Cass

Spiers, E. (2004). *The Victorian Soldier in Africa.* Manchester: Manchester University Press

Spiers, E. (2006). *The Scottish Soldier and Empire 1854–1902.*
    Edinburgh: Edinburgh University Press

Temple, B. & Skennerton, I. (1983). *A Treatise on the British Military
    Martini, Vol. 1: The Martini-Henry 1869–1900.* Burbank:
    B. Temple

Temple, B. & Skennerton, I. (1989). *A Treatise on the British Military
    Martini, Vol. 2: The .40 & .303 Martinis, 1880–c. 1920.*
    Burbank: B. Temple

*Temple, B. & Skennerton, I. (1995). A Treatise on the British Military
    Martini, Vol. 3: Manufacture, Training Arms & Accessories.*
    Kilcoy: B.A. Temple

Vandervort, B. (1998). *Wars of Imperial Conquest in Africa 1830–1914.*
    London: UCL Press

Westwood, D. (2005). *Weapons and Warfare: An Illustrated History of
    their Impact: Rifles.* Oxford: Clio

Woodend, H. (1981). *Catalogue of Enfield Pattern Room Rifles.*
    London: HMSO

INDEX

References to illustrations and plates are shown in **bold**. Captions to plates are shown in (brackets).